Life Lessons from the Lottery:
Protecting Your Money in a Scary World

By Don McNay, CLU, ChFC, MSFS, CSSC
Best-selling author, syndicated columnist, structured settlement
consultant

RRP International LLC

RRP International LLC, DBA Eugenia Ruth LLC
316 Carriage Hill Ct.
Richmond, Ky. 40475

Previous books by Don McNay:
Wealth Without Wall Street
*Son of a Son of a Gambler: Winners, Losers and What to do When
You Win the Lottery*
The Unbridled World of Ernie Fletcher

ISBN-13: 978-0979364426
ISBN-10: 0979364426

Liam Bigler, checking out some of the books grandpa wrote

Most of the wedding party for Don and Karen McNay

In November 2011, my third grandchild Liam Bigler came into the world.

Previous books have been dedicated to Abijah Luhys and Adelaide Bigler, and now Liam gets a book dedicated to him.

I can't wait until he is old enough to read it.

I devoted my *Wealth Without Wall Street* book to my wife Karen, who I married in June 2012, my granddaughter Adelaide and my mentor Al Smith, who is known as the greatest living Kentuckian.

At the rehearsal dinner for our wedding, it struck me that some of my greatest treasures are the friendships I have developed. I won the lottery of life. I have intelligent, successful and honorable friends who are wonderful role models. Most have been close friends for over 30 years and give me loyalty, trust and the knowledge that they will be there when I need them.

In doing my research on lottery winners and people who receive large sums of money, I realize how many are taken in by "friends" who are really looking for a handout.

If they had the kind of true friends that I do, most would still have their money.

Along with Liam, I want to dedicate this book to Clay Bigler, Nick McNay, Mike Behler, Lee Gentry, Bob Babbage and David Grise. They stood up for me on my wedding day and have stood by me for decades.

Don discussing what to do when you win the lottery with Rebecca Jarvis on the *CBS Morning News*

Table of Contents

Table of Contents

Introduction

"I'm just a lonely pilgrim.
I walk this world in wealth
I want to know if it's you I don't trust
'Cause I damn sure don't trust myself"
-Bruce Springsteen

Why do people run through large sums of money quickly?

I've devoted over 30 years of my life finding the answer to this question.

When you hear about Powerball winner Jack Whittaker running through millions that he received from the lottery or Alan Iverson, who has none of the $154 million he made as a professional basketball star, you can't help but wonder what happened.

It's not just famous people who do stupid things with their money. It's everyone.

A report by the National Endowment for Financial Education said that 70 percent who receive a lump sum from any source run through it in a few years.

Many people will deal with a life-changing amount of money at some point in their lives.

They may inherit cash or receive life insurance proceeds. Most have retirement money or a 401k plan. They may get a bonus or buyout at work. They could get an injury settlement or a workers' compensation award.

There are people who hit the lottery, start a successful business or become entertainers and athletes.

No matter the source, there is a universal conclusion: People with big money have a problem holding onto it.

I've wondered why people who can handle monthly paychecks will turn around and blow a large sum.

An insight comes from an unrelated field, Michael Pollan's best-selling book, *In Defense of Food*.

Pollan discussed why high-fructose corn syrup in food can lead to sugar cravings and obesity.

He said, "Human bodies that can cope with chewing coca leaves cannot cope with cocaine or crack, even though the same active ingredients are in all three." Fructose is the "crack" version of corn.

Cocaine and crack hit the body too fast for people to process it.

Big money works the same way. Money that comes to a person fast or in a large amount can overwhelm them.

The Pollan analogy correlates with a fascinating psychological study.

A group of four-year-old nursery school students were part of a study done at Stanford University in the late 1960's.

The children were given the opportunity to eat a marshmallow. Ones who ate it immediately only received one marshmallow. The ones who waited for an undetermined time (up to fifteen minutes) would receive a second marshmallow.

Most of the children couldn't wait. Most grabbed and ate the first marshmallow immediately.

The psychologist tracked the participants over the next 40 years. The children who waited for the second marshmallow went on to live productive and, in many cases, outstanding lives.

Those who immediately grabbed a marshmallow didn't do as well.

Walter Mischel, the Stanford psychology professor who did the study, got serious about tracking the students in 1981. He studied every trait he could think of.

The students who couldn't wait were more prone to adult behavior problems and inability to deal with stress.

When they got to college age, the nursery school students who waited 15 minutes averaged SAT scores 215 points higher than those who could only wait 30 seconds.

Mischel may have discovered the Rosetta Stone of why some people become wealthy and others do not.

Dr. Thomas Stanley has done extensive research into why some people become millionaires. His book *The Millionaire Next Door* was a huge bestseller.

Stanley noted that education and intelligence did not automatically predict wealth. He said that small business owners, without advanced degrees, were more likely to be millionaires than were doctors or lawyers.

It has always amazed me how some well-educated people make stupid mistakes with their money. Now I understand. They were the people who couldn't wait for the marshmallow.

The Stanford scientists are studying genetics and are trying to learn if some regions of the brain assist in delaying gratification. The study gives credence to the idea that people who "can't help themselves" really can't help themselves. Something in their DNA makes it harder for some people to delay getting a reward.

Those who are prone to grabbing need to restrict access to the marshmallow.

The marshmallow analogy is one piece of the puzzle. Over 30 years, I've worked with injury victims, lottery winners or people getting an inheritance. Despite my best efforts, I've watched many blow through it. I've concluded that people blow through money for five different reasons.

1. Family and friends. People try to "buy" love and friendship or they feel compelled to show off by buying houses, cars, clothes and items. As Will Rogers used to say, "They are spending money they don't have to impress people they don't know."

2. Bad habits, bad advisors, lack of knowledge. People who spend more than they make will not suddenly be "cured" when they get a lump sum of money. In fact, whatever problems they had will now be magnified by having more money to get in more trouble with.

3. Taking the money in a lump sum. Social security, defined benefit pension plans and many other programs pay out money over a lifetime instead of in a lump sum. They know that people will run through a lump sum quickly and become broke. I'm in the structured settlement and annuity business and have been successful as I am not a peddler of products; I am a hardcore, true believer. The people who are happiest in my role are those who have a monthly check coming in that they can count on.

4. They don't think before they act. People make impulse decisions. They think they can pay something off "over time." Then time runs out on their money.

5. Not having a purpose for their money. My father was a professional gambler and owned bars. As a child, it would stun me to see men who had toiled all week in a steel mill or hard labor job come into a bar and gamble a week's pay in one night. The workers knew how to make money, but had no purpose for it.

I wrote a best-selling book about lottery winners. I tell people to do five things if they find out they hit the jackpot.

1. Never tell anyone you won. If you live in a state where you can collect the money anonymously, do so.
2. Talk to experts who have worked with more money than you have. If you win $100 million, find advisors who have received $150 million.
3. Take the money in payments instead of a lump sum.
4. Don't make any quick decisions. Take some time and put together a plan.
5. Use your money for a purpose.

Note the same issues and solutions. No matter how large or small the amount of money you are dealing with.

Having made the connection that people who take a lump sum have the same problems that lottery winners do, I've taken the advice for lottery winners and distilled it into practical advice, commentary and insights that the average person can use.

Life Lessons from the Lottery is not your typical personal finance book. It's not about tweaking a few habits or taking advantage of some change in the tax law. This book is about taking a deep look into your soul, finding out what you are looking for in life and using the money you have to get you there.

Anyone who studied Maslow's hierarchy of needs can understand why people blow through money so quickly. If you are looking for love in all the wrong places, you are never going to hang onto your cash. I see people trying to buy love all the time. Trying to buy love from their spouse, indulging their children, impressing their "friends." It never works.

The Beatles said it best: "Money can't buy me love."

Money can bring you security and allow you to live a comfortable lifestyle. Money can help you provide for your family. Making money can give you a feeling of accomplishment and losing it, a sense of failure.

As Springsteen noted in his song "Brilliant Disguise," many people don't trust themselves. With money or anything else.

After learning lessons from lucky and unlucky lottery winners, people can trust themselves when their financial ship comes in.

That is what this book is about.

The book is broken into five sections. Each section is based on one of the five nuggets of knowledge that I give to lottery winners. I will show how the same concepts apply to anyone who gets money for any reason.

One of my friends describes me as "everyone's favorite uncle" because people come to me with their problems, personal and financial. My solutions stem from a combination of academic study and the school of hard knocks. This book will reflect insights from both worlds.

I have one goal for any person I deal with: Make sure that their money brings them happiness.

Follow the counsel of this book and you will be on your way to achieving your own version of happiness.

With your money and your life.

Lottery Advice

Published on Dec 28, 2009 by abc36tv

December 28, 2009 Greg Stotelmyer

30 likes, 1 dislikes   19,674 views

The Five Things to Do When You Win the Lottery

In 2008, I wrote a best-selling book called *Son of a Son of a Gambler: Winners, Losers and What to Do When You Win the Lottery.* I can boil down my advice to five points:

1. Tell as few people as possible (preferably no one) that you won.
2. Work with a financial advisor who works with more money than you have.
3. Take the money in annual payments instead of the lump sum.
4. Take a deep breath and make some good, long-term decisions. You don't have to cash the ticket today.
5. Use some of the money to give back to society.

Those are five simple rules that about 90 percent of lottery winners don't follow.

1. Tell as few people as possible (preferably no one) that you won.
If you can keep your jackpot quiet, do so. As I told Rebecca Jarvis during an interview on *CBS Morning News*, "Once you have told the world that you received money that you never expected to have, everyone has their hand out, and you are not prepared for it." I once told a young, single, publicly known lottery winner that he had just become the best-looking man in his city. He was realistic enough to know that that wasn't really the case.

2. Work with a financial advisor who works with more money than you have.
There are financial advisors, estate planning attorneys and trust officers who have worked with $100,000,000 or more. The scorekeeper for your local bowling league is not one of them.

People will often hire a friend as opposed to someone who really knows about big money. A good friend would tell you the situation is too complicated for them and help you find some real experts. A lottery winner has tax, estate and planning issues that they didn't have the week before.

3. Take the money in annual payments instead of the lump sum.
Roughly 98 percent of all lottery winners ignore this advice, but I continue to preach the mantra. Taking the payments over time allows you to adjust, with the money coming in on a gradual basis. If you make mistakes and lose all your money the first few years, you have 24 more opportunities to get it right. There are also some tax advantages to taking the money over time, as you are taxed on the money as you receive it. That may not be relevant with $100 million, as you are always going to be in the highest tax bracket, but a person who gets $1 million and takes $50,000 a year might be able to save overall.

4. Take a deep breath and make some good, long-term decisions. You don't have to cash the ticket today.
Some people can't wait to cash their ticket. There have been stories about people camping out in front of lottery offices overnight with the winning ticket. Most lotteries allow you several months or a year to cash a winning ticket. The money will still be there in a month or so. Take some time to figure out what you are going to do with the money and how you are going to do it.

5. Give back to society.
There are many people who have accumulated great wealth, like Rockefeller and Carnegie in the 20th century and Bill Gates and Warren Buffett in this century, who are giving away most of their money during their lifetimes. People who use their wealth to make an impact on society are far happier than those who use it to show off to the neighbors.

The Five Reasons People Blow Their Money

1. Family and friends. People try to "buy" love and friendship or they feel compelled to show off by buying houses, cars, clothes and items. As Will Rogers used to say, "They are spending money they don't have to impress people they don't know."

2. Bad habits, bad advisors, lack of knowledge. People who spend more than they make will not suddenly be "cured" when they get a lump sum of money. In fact, whatever problems they had will now be magnified by having more money to get in more trouble with.

3. Taking the money in a lump sum. Social security, defined benefit pension plans and many other programs pay out money over a lifetime instead of in a lump sum. They know that people will run through a lump sum quickly and become broke. I'm in the structured settlement and annuity business and have been successful as I am not a peddler of products; I am a hardcore, true believer. The people who are happiest in my role are those who have a monthly check coming in that they can count on.

4. They don't think before they act. People make impulse decisions. They think they can pay something off "over time." Then time runs out on their money.

5. Not having a purpose for their money. My father was a professional gambler and owned bars. As a child, it would stun me to see men who had toiled all week in a steel mill or hard labor job come into a bar and gamble a week's pay in one night. The workers knew how to make money, but had no purpose for it.

Don with a man who was never quiet, Muhammad Ali

Rule One: Keep It Quiet

Rule One for Lottery Winners: *Tell as few people as possible (preferably no one) that you won.*

One of the Five Reasons People Blow Their Money: *Family and friends.*

Peer pressure, family pressures and "keeping up with the Joneses" are the most common reasons that people blow a lump sum.

It's also one of the most difficult problems to fix. My four-year-old granddaughter can charm me out of anything. It takes all of my discipline to say no, and I don't do so as often as I should.

We all have a version of my granddaughter in our lives. For some, it can be a romantic interest. For others, it can be family or friends. A lot of people get caught up in trying to impress people with their wealth. I see all kinds of "worthy causes" lining up to get a handout from someone with sudden wealth.

Taking the money anonymously

"I've got two tickets to paradise."
-Eddie Money

"Gonna take your mama out all night. Yeah, we'll show her what it's all about."
-Scissor Sisters

"They whisper, promises in the dark."
-Pat Benatar

Never let anyone know you won the lottery.

Every winner who goes public eventually tells stories about people harassing them.

Powerball winner Jack Whittaker said, "There should be a book to tell you how to handle it when people get thrown into the limelight."

You are asking for trouble if you have a news conference and tell the world that you have a bunch of money that you never planned on having.

The best way to hang on to your money is not let anyone know you have it. That can be tough for lottery winners. Each state has its own rules on whether you can collect the money anonymously. Ohio and several other states allow you to do so, while states like Florida make you have a news conference before you can accept your money.

The news conference turns out really well for the lottery officials promoting their product, and it provides a good story for the media. It will not, however, turn out so well for the winner.

I've thought about starting a group called "Lottery Winners Anonymous" to compel all 50 states to allow lottery winners to avoid the spotlight.

After the "death by lottery" of Abraham Shakespeare, Florida would be my first stop.

Shakespeare even had a tragic name.

Abraham Shakespeare should have been on top of the world. In 2006, he won $16.9 million in the Florida lottery.

A few years later, they found his body. Buried five feet deep and under concrete.

His death wasn't a big surprise. He had been missing since April, but no one bothered to report him missing until November 9.

Shakespeare had acquired a huge entourage, but they didn't really miss him. They just missed his money.

I hope Mr. Shakespeare is now in heaven. From the day he stood in front of a news conference, holding a big replica of a Florida lotto check, his life became a living hell.

Like every other lottery winner, Shakespeare said the money wouldn't change him. Like every other lottery winner, it did.

Not for the better.

Right off the bat, one of Shakespeare's coworkers sued, claiming that Abraham had stolen the winning ticket from him. The jury ruled for Shakespeare six months later, but by then, according to the New York Daily News, "there were people constantly asking for a piece of his fortune."

Dorice Donegan "Dee Dee" Moore was a person who may have taken a good chunk of it.

Moore was charged with first degree murder concerning Shakespeare's disappearance and death.

It seemed like everyone wanted a piece of Shakespeare. According to published reports, Dee Dee Moore had a joint bank account with Shakespeare and acquired nearly $2 million of his money. Shakespeare did not find Moore. She found him. By hunting him down. Troy McKay Young, a Lakeland, Florida police officer, was arrested for unlawful compensation, as he was alleged to have sold confidential information such as Shakespeare's license plate number to Dee Dee Moore.

If Shakespeare had been able to keep out of the media spotlight, he might still be with us.

Amanda Clayton was not your typical millionaire. In her short, 25-year life, she won a million dollar lottery, was convicted of collecting state welfare money AFTER she got the million dollars and was embroiled in a plethora of drama and legal battles.

In her home state of Michigan, it's possible for state lottery winners to collect their winnings anonymously, except for Mega Millions and Powerball winners.

Thus, Amanda would have been better off to quietly take her winnings, but it didn't work out that way.

If you go online, you can find a happy and attractive Amanda from September of last year. She was smiling, holding a huge million dollar check from the Michigan Lottery.

Now she is in a coffin, holding a lily. For eternity. The big check and lily are correlated. She lived a troubled life. Getting the lottery money added rocket fuel to her problems.

From various news accounts, it seemed like Amanda had a ton of newfound "friends." All wanting to take advantage of her.

Although Amanda was not shy about making headlines with her check, she "forgot" to mention it to one group of people: the food stamp and public assistance office.

According to *The Detroit News*, Clayton pled no contest to fraud in June after state prosecutors accused her of receiving $5500 in food and medical benefits after she won the lottery.

Millionaires are not supposed to collect food stamps. If Amanda had tried to rip off the government as a Wall Street banker, her crime would have been ignored and she probably would have received a government bailout.

She got nine months probation instead. She wound up not staying alive until the end of her sentence.

It's sad to see a 25-year-old throw their life away. I'm not sure that winning the lottery was the source of her problems, but I see it happen too many times.

People who win the lottery lose perspective on normal things in life. They start to think that rules don't apply to them. In Amanda's case, she thought she could outsmart the welfare people and do serious drugs without consequence.

She lost her bet both times.

Some people want to collect their money anonymously, but don't understand how to do it.

Linville Lee Huff of Bullitt County, Kentucky was outed.

The outing had nothing to do with his personal life. He wanted to be a closet Powerball winner, but is now a public figure.

Huff was the winner of a Powerball jackpot. He claimed the cash option of $16.8 million.

Mr. Huff had requested to the Kentucky Lottery that his winning ticket remain anonymous. Instead, Huff's name was obtained by the *Louisville Courier Journal* and published after the *Courier Journal* made an open records request.

Linville Lee Huff will forever be known as Linville Huff, Powerball winner.

Mr. Huff had good intentions about keeping his winnings quiet. He implemented those intentions poorly.

A man who just got $16.8 million should have spent some of that cash on good advice. Any sudden millionaire, Powerball winner or not, needs to bring in expert consultants.

Huff could have avoided the mad rush of friends, strangers, charities and freeloaders looking for a piece of his money.

After the *Courier Journal* disclosed Huff's name, some readers took umbrage with the newspaper. It was not the *Courier Journal*'s duty to help Mr. Huff protect his identity. They are not in the business of providing free advice to millionaires.

The *Courier Journal* is a news gathering organization. Mr. Huff's identity was news. Huff did not take proper steps to protect himself.

Huff seemed to have good intentions and the right idea. It gets more complicated as many lottery winners WANT to be famous. I'm not sure why the idea of picking a number makes someone feel intelligent or privileged, but many can't help seeking the spotlight.

There are millions of people who want to be on reality television or appear on *Jerry Springer*. I don't understand them, but I know they exist.

Thus, there will always be lottery winners who want to flash their wealth. In fact, there are several people who did not actually win the lottery, but wanted people to think they did.

A few years ago, a woman in Cleveland filed a police report claiming that she had lost a $162 million lottery ticket. Although she had had an extensive police record, some people gave her story credence—until the real winner came forward.

The woman tried to divert attempts at justice by saying she lied in order to help her children as well as unemployed Cleveland police officers.

Since Cleveland policemen have handcuffed her and hauled her away in the past, I am not sure why she claimed she wanted to split her winnings with them. It could be that she hoped to get some special treatment the next time she was arrested. She might have been looking for police protection from the throngs of people who believed her story and started searching her neighborhood in order to find the missing ticket.

One of the most bizarre lottery winner stories in recent years comes out of Shelbyville, Indiana. A man claimed to have won a $34.5 million jackpot and supposedly went to great lengths to hide it from the wife he was divorcing.

Then the lawyer for an anonymous woman, said to be over 70 years old, stepped forward to say his client was the winner.

The poster child for why lottery winners should never be in the media is Powerball Jack Whittaker of Hurricane, West Virginia.

On Christmas Day, 2002, Whittaker won nearly $315 million in the Powerball jackpot, which was at the time the largest individual Powerball jackpot ever.

He did the big news conference and his story received worldwide publicity. Then his life went to hell.

Usually you read about millionaires on the business page. Jack made regular appearances in another part of the paper: the police blotter.

While he was hanging out at a strip club, someone put a drug in his drink and took $545,000 in cash that he had sitting in his truck. He was charged with bouncing checks in casinos. He has been sued numerous times for numerous reasons. He was arrested on drunk driving charges. He has been charged with assault.

Most tragically, his granddaughter died of a drug overdose after being indulged for her every whim by her grandfather. Prior to that, one of her friends died of a drug overdose in Whittaker's house.

After 42 years of marriage, Whittaker's wife divorced him in 2008. She was quoted as saying that she "wished they had torn up the ticket." The divorce spawned a bitter legal battle that was decided by the West Virginia Supreme Court in 2011.

It's hard to attribute all of Jack's problems to the glare of accepting the money in the spotlight of the media frenzy.

Jack was a 65-year-old, self-made millionaire in the construction business before he won the lottery. He had been in a long and stable marriage and appeared to be a loving father and grandfather. He was not an obvious pick to go completely crazy.

But like many Hollywood stars who get a taste of the spotlight and push the envelope to stay in it, something about getting all the attention can bring out the worst instincts in people and especially the worst instincts in people around them.

Thus, keeping it quiet is rule one for anyone winning the lottery.

Don's parents, "Bingo Joe" and Ollie McNay, at the Latin Quarter in Newport, Kentucky, with four of their dearest friends, looking like a scene right out of a *Godfather* movie

Keep your friends not so close and enemies even further away

"Keep your friends close, but your enemies closer."
-Michael Corelone (Al Pacino) in *The Godfather Part II*.

"Tell me who your friends are, I'll tell you who you are."
-Bingo Joe McNay (my father), a professional gambler and bookmaker.

"Don't stand so close to me."
–The Police

A friend recently lost her husband at a young age. She told me that men started coming on to her at the funeral. I see it all the time.

The first thing I tell lottery winners, widows, widowers or others who come into large sums of money is to watch out for their family and especially for newfound "friends."

The line in *The Godfather II* about keeping your friends close and your enemies closer works the opposite for people with sudden money. People are usually smart enough to keep their enemies at bay, but it's often the friends who are grabbing for their wallet.

Things get really complicated when someone is going through a life change. I hit the trifecta several years ago when, within six months, my mother and sister died suddenly and my first marriage ended.

Life was out of balance and I made a lot of silly mistakes, especially when I went back into the dating pool.

Everyone thought I would fall for someone who only wanted my money. I had lots of bad experiences, but having someone take me for my money was not one of them.

Some of it was luck. My first relationships were with well-educated professionals with plenty of family wealth. They were looking for someone who wasn't trying to get to their money.

The primary factor that kept me in check was watching hundreds of people walk into my office with lots of money only to come back broke a few years later.

Family and friends were the downfall almost every time.

I've never figured out if family and friends have an "ouch" mark. In other words, they can stay moral and ethical if the "loved one" does not have much disposable income, but "re-evaluate" their ethics if said person comes into a lot of cash.

Most people have friends and companions who are within 15 percent of their own income. When that number gets out of whack, the temptation for the person who has money to use it as a source of control increases, and the temptation of the poorer person to justify being subsidized increases as well.

To quote Glenn Frey, "The lure of easy money has a very strong appeal."

I suspect there is an evil side to some people that turns on whenever they see someone is vulnerable. A law of the jungle that comes forth in humans.

I'm fortunate to have a street-smart family. My father, Bingo Joe, was a professional gambler who was the ultimate creature of the streets. Dad had a mantra: "Tell me who your friends are, and I will tell you who you are."

Dad saw many people brought down by the people they befriended. One of my favorite movies on that theme is Al Pacino's movie *Carlito's Way*, based on two excellent novels (*Carlito's Way* and *After Hours*) by Edwin Torres.

Al Pacino stars as a man trying to break away from his "friends" who ultimately bring him down.

It is a struggle many face in life. The winner inside them can be brought down by friends, family and coworkers.

The worst instincts in people come out when there is money involved.

Selecting friends is a tricky concept.

When my daughter Angela Luhys was in the dating world, she developed a concept that she called the "trailer park test."

When a man tried to impress her with material possessions, she always imagined if she would still like him if he lived in a trailer park instead of a nice house.

If she decided that she would still like the guy if he lived in a trailer park, he stayed. If she decided that his money played into how she viewed him, he went.

Angela, who wants (and deserves) full and total credit for coining the phrase "trailer park test," works with me at the McNay Group, where we deal with injured people, lottery winners and others who come into sudden money.

We realized that the "trailer park test" is not just a dating tool; it is a way to measure how people interact with anyone with money.

You frequently see professional athletes and lottery winners develop a group called "the posse." In Elvis's case, it was called the Memphis Mafia. The posse is a group of hangers-on who tell the wealthy person what they want to hear and hope to have money and reflected glory.

The person who gets a large sum of money should do a "reverse trailer park test" on their potential posse. Ask themselves if the "friends" or new "romantic interest" would still be in their life if they lived in a trailer park.

Going back to my advice for lottery winners, the quieter you are about your money, the better. However, there are some people, such as entertainers and professional athletes, who have to be high profile as part of their profession.

Thus, it is not surprising that friends and family play into their financial woes.

Sports Illustrated did a terrific piece in 2009 titled "Why Athletes Go Broke." The statistics are horrifying. By the time they have been retired for two years, 78 percent of former NFL players have gone bankrupt or are under financial stress because of joblessness or divorce. Within five years of retirement, an estimated 60 percent of former NBA players are broke.

Sports Illustrated cited several reasons why athletes ran through their money, but the "posse" was a big one on the list.

People often make terrible choices when their lives are in upheaval. I see it frequently when people receive money from a family death or injury settlement.

Kathy Trant attracted worldwide attention by quickly spending the $4.7 million she received for the death of her husband, killed in the September 11, 2001 World Trade Center attack.

Trant called the money "blood money." Her spending sprees were a sub-conscious or conscious effort to run through the money. Her "friends" were there to help her.

I've had a number of widowers and widows remarry quickly and then turn all financial decisions over to the new spouse. Usually, the new spouse and the money run out at about the same time.

I had a client whose wife was killed in a car wreck. He got $500,000. I helped him invest his money, but every month the new wife would come to my office wanting to withdraw more. Each time, she was sporting new jewelry, a mink coat and other expensive items. I finally went to their house and told them they were going to run out of money.

They moved their money to another broker. Within six months, she had spent the entire $500,000 and left town.

Kathy Trant can't get the money back from the 30 leeches that she took to the Super Bowl. People who prey on grieving widows don't have the money or conscience to help her. I suspect she subconsciously thinks that getting rid of the money will bring back her husband and her old life.

It's not just people with large amounts who feel like they are taking "blood money."

National headlines came out of Aurora, Indiana in 2007, when a Pizza Hut waitress received a $10,000 "tip" by one of her regular customers.

Buried in the story was an important fact: "Becky," the anonymous woman who left the tip, had just received an injury settlement. Becky's husband and oldest daughter had been killed in an accident.

Becky didn't win the money in a lottery. She received it as compensation for a terrible loss.

The media spin has been to pat Becky on the back for her generosity. The feel-good story is the Pizza Hut waitress's life will be better because of the "tip."

The waitress's "tip" did not come from an emotionally stable business person. It came from someone going through a personal hell.

Giving $10,000 to a semi-stranger is not evidence of sound thinking or long-term financial planning. It shows signs of a hurting person who perceived that her settlement was "blood money."

Although the focus has been on people who are going through dramatic life changes, such as lottery winners and people who lost a loved one, being taken by those supposedly close to someone with money is a universal problem.

I once read that the reason private clubs and country clubs came into fashion was to allow wealthy people a chance to interact with those of similar income. I know many people of extreme wealth, and many keep it by being constantly mistrusting those around them.

Living life in constant suspicion of your family and friends doesn't sound like fun either.

Some simple rules for friendship to prevail:

1. Never lend money to anyone. You are a person, not a bank.

Follow the advice of William Shakespeare. In Hamlet, Lord Polonius said, "Neither a borrower nor a lender be; For loan oft loses both itself and friend, And borrowing dulls the edge of husbandry."

In modern terms, "Friends don't borrow money from friends. That is what banks are for."

In a world of banks, automobile financing, mortgage brokers, credit cards, payday lenders, pawn shops and "buy here/pay here" car lots, someone intent on borrowing money can find a professional lender willing to give them money at a rate suitable to their credit history.

They don't need to borrow from their friends.

Most of the time, the friend subconsciously (or even consciously) considers the loan a "gift" and, as Shakespeare noted, it usually ends the friendship.

Like most people, I've been burned on lending money. The last person I lent money to (several years ago) was a very close friend who makes big money. This person also had big issues I did not know about. I lent an amount I could afford. I thought it was on a short-term basis. I've never seen a dime in repayment and rarely see the friend anymore.

We all make that mistake once or twice in our lives. Anyone who has not done it, please jump up and do a cartwheel. You are a distinct minority.

The key is to learn from mistakes. I did. I don't lend money to anyone. I don't cosign either. My children have a similar philosophy.

People will make you think you are a jerk when you turn them down. Actually the opposite is true. Not lending money is more likely to prolong a friendship than lending it.

2. If someone needs an expensive gift to be your friend, they are not actually your friend.

I felt sorry for Michael Jackson. He was a star from early childhood and never got to meet normal people. He was always surrounded by a large entourage, but always had to pay for them to go places. Or pay them a salary.

I have friends in all walks of life. Some possess genius level IQ's and some don't. Some are multi-millionaires and some have to save up to go to lunch at a fast food restaurant. The key is that, for whatever reason, we enjoy each other's company.

It can be tough for people with money to make friends. Like the Eagles song "Lyin' Eyes" says, "a big old house can get lonely," and having money as a measure of control makes it tempting for wealthy people to "buy" people to hang out with.

On the other hand, if you have to buy your friends, you are getting what you pay for. Life is better when you find real people who want your company and not your wallet.

3. If you like hanging out with wealthy people, pick up the check when you dine with them.

My father made good money, but when he died in 1993, he was not a man of great wealth. The average net worth of his pallbearers went well into the millions. Dad's close friend, Hall of Fame disc jockey Jim LaBarbara, said that "Big Joe McNay was bigger than life. He was friends with everyone from (Johnny) Bench and Pete (Rose) to the big politicians. I think he introduced me to half the people in town (Cincinnati), everyone seemed to like him."

Dad was always the first to grab a check and never forgot his friends' birthdays. Many people expect to be "treated" when they are dining with a wealthy person. I've actually seen people order the most expensive things on a menu when they think someone with more income is paying. It's amazing how some can have "short arm disease" when the check arrives.

Dad was the opposite. He found that wealth was one byproduct for people living interesting lives. He was glad to pick up the tab to be in their inner circle. He was the kind of friend a wealthy person wants to have. Thus, his world was filled with them.

4. Friendship is a lifelong journey, not a drive-by experience.

My book is dedicated to my grandson and my friends who stood up for me at my wedding. The men have all had successful careers and are wonderful role models for children.

They have also been my friends for many decades. Even if I don't talk to them for months, I always feel a deep connection.

I am confident that if I won the lottery, none of them would be looking for a handout. All of them would be happy for me. Just like I would be for them.

I meet people who seem to trade in their friends for a new group every year or so. They try to be with the "in crowd" or never get too deep into getting to know someone.

All relationships require trust, love, giving, commitment and flexibility. People who have totally invested in their relationships are less likely to fall prey to an "entourage" or "posse" wanting their money.

Since family and friends are the primary reasons that people blow a lump sum, if you can invest in good quality relationships, you can go a long way toward maintaining financial success as well.

Tuesday

October 10, 2000

Business Editor: Jacalyn Carfagno
Phone: (859) 231-1408
To report a news tip: Call
231-3200 or toll-free at (800) 950-6397
hlbusiness@herald-leader.com

Business

LEXINGTON HERALD-LEADER

One Company's Story

DAVID STEPHENSON/STAFF

Don McNay usually helps people who have won a large sum of money for either a crippling injury or perhaps from a lawsuit. Under its ethics policy, his company cannot solicit business, but clients keep coming.

Rule Two: Find Professional Help

Rule Two for Lottery Winners: *Work with a financial advisor who has worked with more money than you have.*

One of the Five Reasons People Blow Their Money*: Bad habits, bad advisors, lack of knowledge.*

"I will provide for you, and I'll stand by your side.
You'll need a good companion now, for this part of the ride."
-Bruce Springsteen

After more than 30 years of helping people with their money, I figured out long ago that financial issues were rarely about rates of return or asset allocation.

Money is usually about emotions. Most of the time, people are using money to buy something that is missing in their lives.

It could be they are missing love, self-esteem or security. They could be using money to cure loneliness or, as Jackson Browne once said, "to fill in the missing colors of their paint by number dreams."

Most of the time, money doesn't cure what really ails them. The ailment remains, but they wind up losing their money too.

People need help in finding out where they want to go and how to get there.

My solution is simple: Find advisors who have worked with more money than you have. If you win $100 million in the lottery, find advisors who have worked with $150 million.

I would think that solution would solve a lot of problems, but getting people to the right advisors, or any advisors, can be complicated.

There is a great disconnect in the financial world.

A comprehensive Financial Capability Study by The FINRA Investor Education Foundation said that 67 percent of Americans rated their own financial knowledge as "very high."

This is a primary reason that people blow through their money so quickly. They don't know what they are doing, but are convinced that they do.

By the time they figure out their lack of knowledge, they are broke.

The second thing that the FINRA study noted is that only 28 percent would "trust financial professionals and accept what they recommend." It then said that 51 percent agreed with the statement, "Financial professionals are too expensive for me."

In short, people don't trust financial professionals, don't want to pay for a financial professional and think they know what they are doing already.

The financial professionals know there are plenty of people who really need help, but they often do a poor job in marketing their services.

There are a lot of product peddlers who mask themselves as advisors. There are a lot of advisors who don't give a perception of knowledge and trust.

On the other hand, people need help. From somebody.

Going back to the FINRA study, it said that 20 percent of the population spends more than their income. Sixty-two percent did not compare features when getting a credit card. Fifty-eight percent of non-retirees have not tried to calculate how much they will need for retirement. Forty-five percent of retirees didn't try to figure out how much they would need before retiring.

The dueling statistics remind of the Steve Goodman song "Banana Republic," which was a hit for Jimmy Buffett. A line in the song says, "You know that you cannot trust them, 'cause they know they can't trust you."

There are good reasons for having a financial advisor. The reason I hire a mechanic is that I don't know anything about car engines and don't plan to learn. There are people who don't know anything about money and don't want to learn.

I found a great mechanic by asking people who loved cars which mechanic they used. The referral method works in any kind of situation.

The best way to find a financial advisor is to ask someone with lots of money to recommend one.

During media interviews, I tell lottery winners that they should consult with an attorney before doing anything else. That is good advice for most people. Lawyers can set the foundation for good financial and estate planning.

As much as people disconnect with financial professionals, it is even worse with attorneys.

Every year since 1991, the Gallup Organization has polled Americans on which profession they consider the most honest and ethical. When nurses are on the list, they always come out on top, except in 2001 when firefighters, understandably, took the distinction.

Lawyers always run near the bottom, ahead of lobbyists, car salespeople and members of Congress, but behind reporters, bankers and auto mechanics.

Love them or hate them, if you plan to make money and keep it in the family after you die (or if you want to make sure your favorite charities get some cash), you need to develop a relationship with an attorney. It will save you a lot of grief in the long run.

Lawyers can help you with business disputes and tax questions. They can make sure your business and real estate purchases are set up correctly. Lawyers can help you plan what happens to you or your family if you should suddenly die or become disabled. And, even more importantly, they can make sure those plans are carried out. Lawyers can help if you are in an accident. They can help if you are being sued or jerked around by creditors. Lawyers can help if someone owes you money and won't pay.

I've watched people make serious life decisions without using lawyers. That usually doesn't work well. I've seen people pay unnecessarily large chunks in taxes (usually along with penalties and interest) because they didn't ask a lawyer about a transaction. I've seen property disputes arise that didn't need to happen, simply because people didn't use attorneys to draw up proper deeds, leases and agreements.

One such dispute stirred up so much acrimony between neighbors that one shot and killed the other. The shooter then hired a lawyer to represent him in the murder trial. I've watched people negotiate accident settlements with insurance companies and get far less than a good trial attorney would have gotten for them.

I've seen people get burned because they drew up employment contracts or business agreements without an attorney to help them. I've watched people, sometimes extremely wealthy people, lose everything because they co-signed or guaranteed loans and didn't ask an attorney to guide them through the pitfalls.

Often when a person avoids using an attorney, he winds up hiring one later to straighten out the mess. It's like the last time I tried to fix my car without a mechanic. I turned a $50 problem into a $500 one.

I encourage people to use an attorney when they start their own business. I hope the same people become so successful that they eventually need tax and estate planning attorneys to set up trusts to protect their assets and fund worthwhile charities.

Most of us need someone to double check decisions and keep us from making serious mistakes. That is the thing that lawyers do well.

One thing a lawyer might point out is the pitfalls of being separated, but not divorced.

My wife once walked into a gas station and said she was buying a lottery ticket. I told her the odds were 176,000,000 to one. She said that if she won, she would keep the money to herself.

I explained that if she won, half of the jackpot is mine. A winning lottery ticket is a marital asset to be split equally.

Not everyone knows that.

One of the first lottery winners I ever got to know was the divorcing spouse of a guy who won the lottery. The divorce should have been final months earlier, but he was stalling it out while arguing a minor point about child support.

I'm not sure if he got his way about the child support. I do know that she got several million dollars instead.

For those of us who follow the trials and tribulations of lottery winners, seeing a separated but not yet divorced couple hit the lottery has happened more than once.

This makes me think there are a lot of separated couples all over America.

Various census statistics say two to three percent of Americans (roughly six or seven million people) are separated, but don't have their divorce final.

My lottery winner was a great example of why living separate but still married can blow up from a financial standpoint, but an excellent 2010 *New York Times* article, titled "The Un-Divorced," argues the opposite point.

People frequently live apart and stay married for financial reasons.

The *New York Times* article noted one of the most famous separated but not divorced couples: billionaire Warren Buffett and his late wife Susan. They separated in 1977 and stayed that way until Susan's death in 2004. Warren lived with another woman, whom he married after Susan's death, and Susan often made public appearances with Buffett.

I suspect that someone as financially savvy as Warren Buffett had thought through the financial ramifications of his situation, but the average person does not.

Just like the average lottery player does not think about how being married but living separately will impact their situation.

Holly Lahti in Idaho won $190 million in the Mega Million's jackpot in 2011. She has zealously attempted to protect her privacy, but wound up making headlines as she was in the "separated but married" category. Her husband, an ex-con with over a dozen arrests on his record, came looking for his part of the loot. His first reaction was "I won't have to pay child support," and according to a document obtained by RaderOnline.doc, that is exactly what happened.

Holly waived child and medical support for the children. It doesn't say what she received in return.

Few people will ever win the lottery, but financial issues and dilemmas face anyone who is living separately but divorced.

Do you need an adult babysitter?

"I need you, by me, beside me, to guide me,
To hold me, to scold me, 'cause when I'm bad,
I'm so, so bad."
-Donna Summer

"The devil made me do it the first time,
The second time I done it on my own."
-Billy Joe Shaver

The story of Josh Hamilton and his comeback from addiction has been a fascination of mine.

I wrote a column about Josh when the Cincinnati Reds signed him, but before he had started playing in the major leagues. I had a gut feeling he would make it to the top and he did. I became a huge fan.

It wasn't until *Sports Illustrated* did a feature on Josh a couple of years later that I realized what extreme measures were taken for him to make it in the major leagues.

Josh has gone to the depths of hell, including seven trips to drug and alcohol rehab, but found his way back. Redemption was a combination of faith, his wife, a 12-step program and his coach, Johnny Narron, who served as Josh's adult baby-sitter.

Narron was with Hamilton nearly 24 hours a day. He handled all of Josh's money, including petty cash. He ate with Josh, prayed with him, guarded his hotel room and acted as a shield between Hamilton and temptation.

It's worked. Hamilton is now one of the greatest players in baseball.

A professional athlete has the means and motivation to have an adult babysitter. I'm wondering how many average Americans need the same service.

Joe Nocera, the award-winning columnist for the *New York Times*, is a longtime friend.

In his 1994 classic business book, *A Piece of the Action*, Nocera chronicles the history of personal finance in America. He concluded the moves gave Americans the chance to have their own "piece of the action" controlling their financial destinies.

It stunned me a few years after Joe said that Americans were doing a poor job of handling their newfound freedom. I realized he was right.

Americans were better off when they had a defined-benefit and fixed pension, instead of a 401k, where they are subject to fluctuating markets and their own investment decisions.

Americans were better off when they didn't have access to high-interest credit cards and payday lenders. Americans were better off with a conventional mortgage and 20 percent down payment, instead of a nothing-down subprime loan.

We've had increasing amounts of freedom and haven't done a good job of handling it.

For many years, part of my job had been to act as a financial babysitter for people who receive large sums of money. My success rate is good, but it comes from understanding that people are often going to fall to temptation or do something stupid. I learned to place barriers between people and their money.

At some level, adult Americans are crying out for some kind of supervision, guidance and structure. You can see it happening everywhere.

One of the hottest new occupations is life coaching. People have personal trainers to help them exercise, financial advisors to handle their money and psychologists to talk about life problems.

It is not practical to assign an adult babysitter to every hurting American. Few people have the talents of Josh Hamilton. Even fewer have an employer motivated to maximize those talents.

Whatever they are doing with Josh Hamilton, it is obviously working. I'm a big advocate for individual freedom, but it in areas like addiction and finance, many adults and juveniles would be better off with someone beside them, to guide them.

Because when they are bad, they are so, so bad.

Don with Pete Rose, a man who didn't always listen to good advice, and Hall of Fame disc jockey, "The Music Professor" Jim LaBarbara

Avoiding the advisor who gives lousy advice

One reason that people choose to "go it alone" with their finances is they hear about lousy advisors.

An article in *Sports Illustrated* titled "How (and Why) Athletes Go Broke" has a section about misplaced trust. "According to the NFL Players Association, at least 78 players lost a total of more than $42 million between 1999 and 2002 because they trusted money to advisors with questionable backgrounds."

So how do you avoid getting ripped off?

1. Find an advisor who has worked with more money than you have.

That can be a little complicated. A good advisor will never disclose who their clients are. I had an extremely wealthy person ask me if I would name any clients with his net worth. I did, but I refused to give their names.

He smiled when I refused. It was a test. If I had disclosed their names, I would have disclosed his. He agreed to work with me.

There are a variety of ways to check out advisors, such as government filings and records. Few people do it, but with your nest egg on the line, it is not a bad idea.

2. You find the advisor. Don't let the advisor find you.

Dorice Donegan "Dee Dee" Moore had a unique role as the advisor for Florida lottery winner Abraham Shakespeare. She has also been arrested for his murder.

Troy McKay Young, a Lakeland, Florida police office was also arrested for unlawful compensation, as he was alleged to have sold confidential information such as Shakespeare's license plate number to Moore.

The story is that Moore used the information to meet Shakespeare and offer her services.

Shakespeare needed to find his advisor, not let the advisor find him.

Good professionals are referred by other good professionals. My doctors know the best specialists. If I need foot surgery, they know someone who does that. Same holds true with my auto mechanic. If he can't handle it, he knows someone who can.

A referral is a powerful tool. It means you are vouching for the person being referred.

I frequently refer people who live up to my standards. In the world of estate and financial planning, all the best people normally operate via referral.

Thus, ask a lawyer you trust to recommend an advisor. It's the simplest method I know of.

3. Never settle for less. Spend some time and research to make sure you get a VIP experience from every advisor in your life.

As noted, Abraham Shakespeare did not have much luck in finding a financial advisor. His advisor was charged with his murder.

Lottery winners have the same problems average people do, but the problems are magnified by the large amounts they receive.

People who get lousy financial advice normally don't wind up dead. But they do wind up broke.

You can't easily quantify whether a person is a good teacher, plumber or ballet instructor. You need to ask around and ask people you trust.

I've found good help by letting my Facebook universe know about my needs. I have a large number of Facebook friends, and they usually know someone who knows someone.

It also helps to have an expert do that research for you. I use Anne Parton at iAssist whenever I want to bring a consultant of any sort into my life.

I spent most of the Christmas season of 2011 in the hospital. I made a list of things to do when I got better and playing golf was one of them.

Anne sat down with me, developed a comprehensive list of what I wanted to do as a golfer and how much time I needed to schedule.

Then she went out to interview golf professionals. She came back with Clay Hamrick.

I would have never found Clay on my own. He is the head pro at Battlefield Golf Course, a small public course. Not my first spot to find the ultimate golf guru.

He is a passionate advocate for how golf can improve my overall well-being and physical health. He, Anne and I have an extensive plan for improving my game over the next two years. It also relates to how I am starting to lose weight (40 pounds since I started playing) and do something that does not involve an easy chair.

The key was figuring out what I wanted and finding a top-notch person to implement the plan.

If Abraham Shakespeare had done the same, he might be alive and enjoying his lottery winnings, instead of dying an early death.

4. Never make a "good deal" with a bad person.

Character matters. Trust is the most important component in developing a financial relationship.

That seems obvious, but I constantly run into people who are blinded by a "too good to be true" deal and don't pay attention to who is offering "the deal."

There are some people you do business with and others you don't. Wayne Rogers had a simple way of ferreting them out.

Rogers, best known as Trapper John on the television show *M*A*S*H*, had a second career as an investment and business guru.

According to Rogers, there are four kinds of business deals: good deals with good people, bad deals with bad people, good deals with bad people and bad deals with good people.

The first two are simple: Everyone wants good deals with good people, and no one wants bad deals with bad people.

Regarding the other possibilities, Rogers said that good deals with bad people will always fail and that a bad deal with good people could potentially work out someday.

A bad person will always make a good deal go bad, and a good person might make a bad deal right.

Character is more important than talent, a great deal or promised riches.

It is surprising how many businesses don't get it. Some sports teams don't get it either.

For decades, the Cincinnati Bengals were one of the worst teams in football. It seemed like every year several Bengal players did something stupid or criminal—often both.

The team had several players you would never invite over for dinner, unless you had armed guards around the house.

The Bengals lost games that they should have won. A team with more character would have pulled them out.

That did not happen in the early days. Paul Brown, who founded the Bengals, was a believer in hiring well-rounded players.

When all-pro defensive tackle Mike Reid quit to become a musician, Brown encouraged him to pursue his dream. I don't know if Brown was alive when Reid started receiving Grammy awards, but he would have been proud. Brown had character and looked for players who mirrored his values.

Paul Brown won a lot of games. He is in the football Hall of Fame.

Because they live their lives in the public eye, it is easy to spot character, determination and team spirit in professional athletes. It is a lot harder to spot those traits in businesspeople.

Like everyone in business, I've been burned by bad people that I thought were good. However, I have rarely been burned chasing deals with people I don't trust. I know that there is no such thing as a good deal with a bad person.

Even before Wayne Rogers summed it up, I watched my late father do business as a gambler. In his era, you couldn't sue to enforce a gambling debt. All Dad had was a bettor's word.

It worked for him. In a world where trust was everything, a person's reputation became known quickly.

His philosophy was simple: "Don't do business with liars and cheaters."

It seems like an easy lesson that some people don't get.

I've had people tell me about deals that are too good to be true. It was because they weren't true.

The people peddling them had no history of ever telling the truth. I heard my dad tell a man once, "I judge horses on past performance, and based on your past performance, you are never getting money from me."

It is not that hard to figure out who is good and who is bad. Some people will fool you, but if you do some homework and be realistic in your expectations, you will rarely get burned.

If a football player or a businessperson has a history of being a troublemaker, they will be a cancer to those around them. They will bring the good players down to their level.

Like in business, the Bengals should see that when faced with a "great deal" from someone with a dubious reputation, just keep walking.

5. Find advisors who really care about their customers.

"I deal in dreamers and telephone screamers.
 Lately, I wonder what I do it for.
 If I had my way, I'd just walk through those doors."
-Joni Mitchell

Joni Mitchell's 1974 song "Free Man in Paris" was about record company president David Geffen and the pressures he faced.

Geffen is now a billionaire. I wonder if he deals with telephone screamers now. I can't imagine that Geffen is sitting around taking customer service calls.

In fact, I wonder how many people are still taking customer service calls. Many companies have written off the idea. Their phone systems start with a recording that tells you to listen to 20 different options.

Once you get through the options, you are directed to a website where nothing pertains to your problem. If you insist on staying on the phone, after a three-hour wait you are routed to someone in a foreign country who does not speak English. That person mumbles and transfers you back to where you started so that you can begin the whole process anew.

Every time you hear of a corporate merger or downsizing, look for job cuts in customer service. It is a way to show quick profits. Managers think they can get away with bad service and customers won't notice.

There are some companies, however, that still believe in customer service. I work hard to find them.

My method is to find a main contact at places where I do business. No matter what my problem is, I want to deal with just one person.

In my mind, I am not doing business with a company; I am doing business with my contact person. Companies that let me choose my contact person get lots of business from me. Companies that try to make me fit into their bureaucratic structures do not.

One of my favorite companies is Symetra Life Insurance Company in Seattle, formerly known as Safeco Life. I served on their agents' advisory board and came to know everyone in the company, from the president on down. They have many great people at Symetra, but my special contact started as our customer service representative. Our office went to her for every little problem, and she solved it every time. To us, Symetra Life was not a billion-dollar corporation; it was our friend, Sheila Holdt.

She was promoted to a management position in a different department, but for many years, Symetra arranged for her to remain our contact person. It worked for us and worked for her, too.

Symetra understood their customer. It wreaked havoc on some manager's flow chart, but it was a smart business decision.

There is a great book called *What They Don't Teach You at Harvard Business School* by the late Mark McCormick. McCormick started his career as the business manager for Arnold Palmer. If Palmer needed a new golf club, McCormick got it for him. Even after McCormick's business became the biggest sports management company in the world, he would still give Palmer personal attention.

Symetra and McCormick understood that successful businesses really know their customers and pay attention to what they want. It is a simple concept, but too many businesses try to ignore it.

One of the reasons that David Geffen became successful was that he always took care of the small needs of his clients. When Linda Ronstadt or Elton John called him, he did not make them listen to recordings or transfer the call to someone in India. Geffen took the calls and made sure his clients were happy.

He is a good model for advisors to follow. Joni Mitchell's song focused on the pressures Geffen felt in 1974, but now that he is a billionaire, Geffen can be a "Free Man in Paris" or anywhere else he chooses.

A lifetime annuity would have been a good idea for Tony Bennett. This shot was taken after the 86-year-old performed a 90-minute concert in 2012.

Rule Three: Avoid the Lump Sum

Rule Three for Lottery Winners: Take the money in annual payments instead of the lump sum

One of the Five Reasons People Blow Their Money: Taking the money in a lump sum

"Now, baby we can do it.
Take the time, do it right.
We can do it, baby.
Do it tonight."
-The S.O.S. Band

"I want somebody who will spend some time, not come and go in a heated rush."
-The Pointer Sisters

Taking money over time is a tenet of my faith. I believe in God, the Cincinnati Reds and not taking money in a lump sum.

I've spent more than 30 years in the structured settlement business, encouraging people to take payments over time. Watching thousands of people blow through lump sum payments made me a true believer in the power of lifetime income.

Roughly 98 percent of lottery winners ignore my advice. Thus it is no surprise that most of them blow the money in five years or less.

The same statistic holds true for people getting money from an injury settlement, inheritance or retirement. It doesn't make a difference if it is $10,000 lump sum or a $10 million lump sum. People blow through the money.

It makes sense when you think about it. People are used to having money come in every month.

Mortgages, utilities and almost every kind of bill payment are done monthly. People get paychecks on a bi-weekly or monthly basis. They get social security and defined benefit pension payments on a monthly basis.

Thus, managing a lump sum is a completely foreign skill. As survey after survey shows, most people don't do well.

Taking lottery payments over time allows you to adjust with the money coming in on a gradual basis. If you make mistakes and lose all your money the first few years, you have 24 more opportunities to get it right.

I've watched several lottery winners become miniature version of Powerball Jack Whittaker and do silly things the first year or so. If they have a couple of years to adjust, they eventually settle down and enjoy the money.

There are also some tax advantages to taking lottery money over time, as you are taxed on the money as you receive it. That may not be relevant with $100 million, as you are always going to be in the highest tax bracket, but a person who gets $1 million and takes $50,000 a year should be able to save.

When I worked as a Series 7 registered representative (often referred to as a "stockbroker"), I had a large clientele of doctors, lawyers and other well-educated professionals, along with injured people and the occasional lottery winner.

I had my clients allocate their money into several types of investments and did my best to keep them from panicking when one class of investments did poorly.

Over the years, I kept noticing one thing: People who had easy access to cash were the ones most likely to fall off the bandwagon. They would have "emergencies," such as wanting to buy a new car, a houseboat or taking their friends on a cruise. Sooner or later, the money would be gone.

In the meantime, I had a parallel business that provided structured settlement annuities to injured people. Structured settlements are only offered to injury victims and are tax-free. Thus, they are an attractive choice compared to taxable alternatives.

A structured settlement annuity can be designed in a number of different ways, but the way I normally recommend is to pay it out over a person's lifetime, increasing at two or three percent a year to keep up with inflation and guaranteed for 30 years to a beneficiary in case the person dies.

One of my first clients was a young man who lost his arms and legs in an accident and lived with a motorcycle gang. He received roughly $3 million. If he and the motorcycle gang had gotten their hands on $3 million dollars, they would have had the party to end all parties until the money was gone.

I set him up so that he received $10,000 a month.

Thus, they had a party every month up until he died many years later.

You can't really "cash in" a structured settlement, although some people make the unfortunate decision to sell their payments to companies that heavily advertise on daytime television shows such as *Jerry Springer*.

Because the money was harder to access, the people who took structured settlements were more likely to have a stable and happy life than clients who could cash in a mutual fund or stock whenever they wanted.

I realized the psychology was like dieting. I struggle with my weight and used to start a diet about once a month. If I start, but have all my favorite foods in the refrigerator, I will fall off the diet immediately.

If I have to drive to the store about two miles away, I think about it more and sometimes won't go. If I have to drive 25 miles to get fatty foods, I am far more likely to stick to the diet.

The financial analogy is that having all your money in a savings or checking account is like having food in the refrigerator. Putting money in a mutual fund or certificate of deposit, where it takes some effort (and sometimes penalties and tax consequences) to cash it in, is similar to driving to the store two miles away. A structured settlement is like the 25-mile drive for food. You have to do a lot of work to sell it and take a huge financial hit when you do.

It is better just to hang on to the structured settlement and stay disciplined, just like it is better to stay on a diet.

Eventually, I moved away from a successful career as a stockbroker and focused all my efforts on the structured settlement business.

Although many of my eggs are in the structured settlement basket, it was closer to the Will Rogers' philosophy of being concerned about return *of* my money as opposed to return *on* my money.

There is something similar to a structured settlement called an immediate annuity. It pays income for a person's life, just like a defined benefit pension plan. Although people seem to like lifetime income from a retirement plan, a *Smart Money* article stated what I long suspected: Few people buy them on their own.

I never understood why until I read an article called "The Annuity Puzzle" in a June 2011 edition of the *New York Times*.

Dr. Richard Thaler, a professor of economics and behavioral science at the University of Chicago, discussed how purchasing an immediate annuity with 401k retirement money, with fixed and guaranteed benefits, was a simple and less risky option than self-managing a portfolio or having the people on Wall Street do it for you.

He also noted that not enough people buy annuities.

Thaler suggested that people seemed to consider an annuity a "gamble" that they would live to an old age instead of realizing that "the decision to self-manage your retirement wealth is the risky one."

As people live longer than previous generations, they are more likely to run out of money before they run out of time on the earth.

The biggest objection that I see to annuities is that people are afraid to tie up their money. Thaler confirmed what I had long suspected. People are much better off restricting access to their money than having full access.

Another big objection has to be the crumbling faith of Americans in large institutions.

In the book *Eat, Pray, Love*, author Elizabeth Gilbert references Luigi Barzini's *The Italians* in explaining why a country that has "produced the greatest artistic, political and scientific minds of the ages" has not become a world power.

Barzini's conclusion is that after hundreds of years of corruption and exploitation by foreign dominators, Italians don't trust political leaders or big institutions.

Gilbert said the prevailing thought is that "because the world is so corrupted, misspoken, unstable, exaggerated and unfair, one should only trust what one can experience with one's own senses."

She added, "In a world of disorder and disaster and fraud, only artistic excellence is incorruptible. Pleasure cannot be bargained down."

If the mindset of the United States becomes more like the Italians, the concept of thinking long-term will be harder and harder to achieve.

Many lottery winners have the false assumption that payments taken over time will stop if they die before the payments are made. All lotteries allow the payments to go to a beneficiary or loved one. Many annuities allow for payments to a beneficiary as well.

An annuity is just one tool, just like balancing your money among a number of different investments, but the key to wealth is to develop good savings and spending habits.

I've had a successful career in the structured settlement business, primarily because I believe so strongly in the concept. When I meet potential clients, they sense my passion and enthusiasm.

Several years ago, I worked with a large number of people who were injured or killed in the same accident. About half of the people who received money took some of it as a structured settlement. The other half took the money in a lump sum.

I kept up with the group closely. The details of the settlements are confidential, but I don't think that anyone who received a lump sum still has any of it left. Most ran through it in a couple of years. The people who took the structured settlement are very happy. I keep in regular touch with some of them, and they frequently thank me.

Not everyone agrees with Thaler about annuities.

When Brett Arends was at the *Wall Street Journal* in 2008, he wrote a column titled "Take the Money and Run." He said that lottery winners should take the lump sum instead of annual payments.

It was terrific advice for someone who lives in a vacuum or on a desert island. It was bad advice for lottery winners.

Arends made some economic points. He said that taking the lump sum now would net more than normal. Many lotteries base their lump sum calculations on U.S. Treasury Bonds rates. Arends assumed that taxes will be higher in future years. It is a 50/50 guess.

Anders noted that taking the lottery payments over 20 years would net a 5.7 percent rate of return. In a year when the stock market is in free fall and foreclosures are everywhere, 5.7 percent doesn't sound so bad. Not to Anders. He had one word to describe it to describe the 20-year payout. "Yuck."

This rate would look good to those who blew their lottery lump sum. Right now, they have zero. Anyone getting a guaranteed return of 5.7 percent in 2012 would be jumping for joy.

The biography of Arends said that he had been living in London. He might have missed an American idea called dollar cost averaging.

The concept is simple: Instead of dropping all your money in the market at once, you invest over time, like on a weekly or monthly basis. The returns are usually better than timing the market.

Annual payments from the lottery set up perfectly for dollar cost averaging. If a person was smart and invested each year, the ultimate returns should not cause an observer to say "Yuck."

Anyway, we have established that I am passionate about lifetime annuities. I'm also an advocate of a concept called "getting rich slowly."

My approach toward wealth changed in 1992 when I went to a Vanderbilt University alumni meeting and heard William Spitz, the college's treasurer, give a talk about his book, *Getting Rich Slowly: Building Your Financial Future through Common Sense.*

In the book, Spitz sums up his philosophy in ten principles:

1. There are no guarantees, sure things or free rides.

2. It is not necessary to earn extraordinary rates of return to accumulate a sizeable net worth. The focus should be on earning consistent, reasonable returns while avoiding losses.

3. The key is to structure your program to understand the risks involved and have faith in your program to ride out the tough times without making hasty or costly decisions.

4. Diversification is crucial. Spread your risk.

5. Index funds will usually do as well, or better, than investment advisors or managed mutual funds.

6. Make decisions based on economic performance and not on tax avoidance.

7. You should have the same program for asset allocation, no matter how much or how little you are investing. A person with $5,000 should split it into multiple types of investments, just like a person with $5 million should.

8. Every investor is his own worst enemy. No one is immune from swings in emotion and following the herd. Structure your finances to minimize the chance to make sudden decisions.

9. Minimize costs whenever possible.

10. Too much trading and moving money is expensive and counterproductive. To quote Spitz, "The primary beneficiary of a high level of trading is your broker." Set up your portfolio carefully, review it annually, stick with the plan and don't panic.

Getting Rich Slowly: Building Your Financial Future through Common Sense is aimed at academia and is not an easy read, but it was an epiphany for me. I had similar thoughts about how to make money, but Spitz summed them up in one book. It has been the cornerstone for all my philosophies since then.

Spitz gave his advice sixteen years before the Wall Street crash in 2008.

People in 2008 who had their money allocated as Spitz suggested—among a variety of stocks, bonds, mutual funds, real estate, and annuities—did much better than people who put their "eggs in one basket."

A lot of people, including many at Wall Street banks, thought real estate could never go down. They put all their money in the real estate market and got burned.

To sum it all up, the best advice for someone getting a lump sum is to the take the money in payments over your lifetime. Put some of the payments each month in a diversified basket of investments along the lines of the *Getting Rich Slowly* book recommendations.

If there is a better way to get rich slowly, I don't know about it.

Special words of wisdom for parents

"Teach your children well."
-Crosby, Stills and Nash

I have three suggestions for parents concerning money:

1. Keep your children from being spoiled rich jerks.

I helped a young child who is being raised by a committee. His single mother was killed in an accident. The child received a large sum of money from his mother's death and lives with extended relatives.

A judge decided to appoint a committee to handle his upbringing and named a non-related attorney as administrator. I advised the committee as to how to handle his finances.

The child comes from a lower-income family, and few of his relatives are well-educated.

When it came to the issue of the child's spending money, the first thing that the administrator decided was that that the child would have to earn his allowance by working with handicapped children and others less fortunate than himself. He also suggested that the child should be involved in youth groups and receive special tutoring.

The boy is going to have a rough time going through life with no parents, and it will be harder still for him to know that he received a huge amount of money because of his mother's death. Helping children with physical handicaps will give him a sense of self-purpose, and it will also force him to recognize that others in life have adversity and learn to deal with it.

Helping other people might keep the child from being a spoiled, rich jerk.

Money can bring power and security, but it also can bring insecurity. People who are rich never know if someone likes them for who they are or for their money. Many develop the attitude that everyone wants something from them, and they are often right.

I grew up hating private country clubs and considered them to be the pinnacle of snobby elitism. I won't join a private club—although in fairness, no private club has ever asked me to join.

As an adult, I can understand why rich people want to hang out with other rich people. In that environment, everyone is of similar financial status and the rich can feel more secure.

In the case of the young boy, the committee decided that he should take golf and tennis lessons. His finances are set for him, and he will receive large payments over his lifetime. He will probably have friends who are well-off, too. Being a golfer and tennis player will allow him to bond with children who grew up with similar wealth.

If you have children, you want to ensure that they are financially secure. There are some steps to making sure that money does not warp them.

1. Don't let them have it all at once. Most people spend a lifetime gathering significant wealth. Getting too much, too young, does not give a person the proper perspective.

2. Make sure they understand it is not easy to come by. Having them earn money, rather than having it given to them, is a good way for them to find out what other people do to feed themselves. I had a friend that grew up wealthy who once complained that he felt deprived because his neighbor was given a chain of gas stations by his parents and he was not. He could not relate to the idea that many people his age were hoping to get a job pumping gas or making change at a gas station, instead of owning one. His perspective on life was warped.

3. Make sure they know money can do good things. Too many people with inherited wealth spend it trying to impress other people with inherited wealth. If your children know they can spend it to make other people's lives better, they will be happier in the long run.

4. Don't let them think in terms of a big inheritance. I have seen many young people waste their lives waiting for a rich relative to die and leave them a big lump sum. The relative would do them a bigger favor by spending the money on their education and setting up a trust or other mechanism to make sure that any inheritance does not come in as a lump sum.

5. Be a good role model. If you give money to charity, your children probably will too. If you volunteer to do things in the community, your children will follow your lead.

If you want to teach your children not to be spoiled, rich jerks, don't act like one yourself.

2. They don't teach your children about money in college. You need to step up to the plate or it is never going to happen.

If they ever let me speak to a college graduation, here is what I am going to tell them:

College seniors enter a world based on economics and without much preparation for what is about to hit them. College is good for many things, but preparing students for "real world" finance is not one of them.

There are three things a college graduate should know about money: How to make it, how to keep it and how to use it to develop a lifestyle that that will give you long-term happiness.

Even when planning on being an entrepreneur and having their own gig, most graduates get experience by working for someone else. They need someone to hire them.

Getting hired is a tricky thing. There are courses, counselors and tons of books devoted to the subject, but I offer students only one piece of advice: "It's all about them, not about you."

Employers hire employees to help employers make more money. They are not interested in accommodating your personal desires unless that somehow happens to coincide with adding to the bottom line.

You need to sell them. They don't need to sell you.

Do potential employers look at your Facebook page and other social networking sites? Of course they do. I have for a long time. It can make or break a person. I don't mind pictures from drunken keg parties. I can only imagine what my Facebook page would have looked like if people carried cameras during my undergrad years (and, of course, had there even been Facebook then…or computers…or electricity). Doing crazy stuff is part of the college experience.

Employers want a hard worker with a positive attitude. The quickest way to NOT get a job is to mouth out online about your former and current employers. I'm stunned when I see examples of where people post negative remarks about their job or boss, usually while they are sitting at the job where they are supposed to be working.

Which leads to the second topic: How to keep the money you make.

The days of lifetime employment are over. Corporations and government entities come in and cut thousands of jobs on a whim. They will invent a computer or robot that does your job. One day, you will wake up and find that someone in India has taken your position.

Be ready and build a "take this job and shove it" fund. Former Treasury Secretary Don Regan called it "f___ you money."

Either way (though I prefer the Regan terminology), it means freeing yourself from staying in a job you hate because you can't afford to quit.

In order to do that, you need to be financially independent. Most college students aren't.

It used to be that students just didn't have any income. Now they have huge debts.

I keep running into the same type of college graduates. They have big credit card debts, student loans outstanding, payments on cars they're upside-down on and looking to buy their first home.

They are never going to have "f____ you" money. They will spend the next 50 years of their lives at the whim of whatever boss, bank or creditor who wants to pull their chain.

Before buying a brand new car or a house, the focus needs to be on paying down debt and getting some savings in the bank.

Somewhere I read that a person's financial style is set by age 27. If a person is a spender at 20, he may get over it by 30. If he is a spender at 30, he probably will be for the rest of his life.

The years after college are the time to be "reborn," in a financial sense. It's a time to set up your life so that money works for you, rather than you working for money.

Class of _____. You are now ready to take on the world.

3. When it comes to children, play the hand that is dealt to you.

My father was a professional gambler. When faced with any kind of crisis, he would say, "You have to play the hand that is dealt you."

In my career as a structured settlement consultant, a number of my clients have been brain-injured or special needs children. Having been at it for over 30 years, many of the children I originally worked with are now adults.

One of the most fascinating things I have seen is that the parents, almost universally, step up to the plate and do what they need to do to make it better for their children.

Being the parent of a special needs child is one of the toughest jobs in the world. It is a lifelong assignment. You don't ship the child out the door at age 18. Or 30. Or 50. Or ever.

The parents are involved until the day they die.

I've dealt with hundreds of parents of special needs children. They take the hand that is dealt to them. And usually turn that hand into aces.

Much comes down to having a positive attitude. Any child, especially a special needs child, forces parents to understand there is a world beyond themselves.

One of my Facebook friends is the parent of a severely injured child and she summed it up perfectly in a post on my Facebook page:

"I think a lot about the phrase from expectant parents 'as long as the baby is healthy.' No one wants their child to suffer or experience a handicap, but the love and bond you feel with that child that was not born healthy is like no other. It gives you a whole new meaning and depth to life that honestly I would not trade."

Having a special needs child could be a burden or a blessing. Parents with healthy children deal with issues like drugs, substance abuse, sexually transmitted diseases and children who grow up to be selfish, lazy and unmotivated.

I see the parents with adult children living at home for no apparent reason. I see grandparents raising grandchildren when the parents are unwilling or unable.

I've seen a lot of people who thought they had a winning hand with healthy children, but wind up "busting out." To raise a special needs child requires a degree of unselfishness and level-headedness that the average person doesn't have.

Parents of a special child understand that you play the hand that was dealt to you.

A pretty good philosophy for all of us.

Don, here with Arianna Huffington, started as a
***Huffington Post* contributor in 2008.**

Rule Four: Take Your Time

Rule Four for Lottery Winners: *Take a deep breath and make some good, long-term decisions. You don't have to cash the ticket today.*

One of the Five Reasons People Blow Their Money: *They don't think before they act. People make impulse decisions. They think they can pay something off "over time." Then time runs out on their money.*

"Wise men say only fools rush in."
-Elvis Presley

"Accidents will happen, they only hit and run. "
-Elvis Costello

"I'm taking my time,
So please don't rush me.
Trying to sort out some things
I didn't know existed"
- Bonnie Raitt

One of my greatest frustrations is watching someone find they have a winning lottery ticket, race to the lottery office like their car is on fire, do a big news conference and proclaim that the lottery is "not going to change their lives."

They jump up and down like participants on a television game show. Not Jeopardy, but a show where you don't need to be smart to participate.

If I could bet on which people I think are going to be broke in five years, I would bet every dime that none of those people have their money five years later.

Financial decisions should never be made on the run. Especially big money financial decisions. There is an interesting paradox.

The larger the amount of money involved, the more decisions there are to be made. On the other hand, the larger the amount of money involved, the more financial vehicles and opportunities available.

Washington is run by rich people. Campaigns are financed by rich people, and laws are written to favor rich people. When you become a rich person, it is time to take advantage of those laws.

Even if you just become 'semi-rich," there are opportunities and advantages for you to reduce your tax rate, make money and hang onto your money.

It comes down to a few simple steps:
1. Get a mental picture of what you want to do for you.
2. Make sure you handle your money in a way for you to achieve your dreams.
3. Use the financial tools available to protect the dream.

Get a mental picture of what you want to do

"And she never had dreams, so they never came true"
-J. Giles Band

I ask everyone the lottery question.

As a structured settlement consultant, I go to mediations and settlement conferences with people who anticipate receiving large sums of money. When people are getting their thoughts about money together, I ask the question.

Forget about today. If you won the lottery, what would you spend the money on?

The initial answers are usually vague, like "invest" or "put money in the bank."

Then, I tell them that when I become a billionaire, I am going to buy the Cincinnati Reds.

When I tell them about my lifelong desire to own the Reds, they start talking about the things that interest them.

The lottery question is a great one from a planning standpoint. Everyone has dreams and desires, but usually in the recesses of their minds. The question gets those dreams and desires on the front burner.

When someone is getting money, the lottery question helps to get their thoughts together.

Some of them have expensive aspirations (owning a NASCAR team comes up frequently), but usually they want things like sending their children to a nice college, buying a particular piece of property or helping their church.

Once we start the conversation, the list gets longer and longer.

My goal is to get people to think long term. They need to clear their heads of the rat race of everyday life.

The lottery question makes that happen.

You don't find many Americans who really think long-term. Many people go through life without developing real goals or good habits.

Someone once said that American businesspeople think quarter to quarter, Japanese think decade to decade and Chinese think century to century. We need to take a lesson from our friends to the east.

I've been asking the lottery question for more than a decade. Not sure, but I could have gotten the original idea from "Strategic Coach" Dan Sullivan. Sullivan is one of my great influences. So many of his teachings are internalized in my way of thinking that sometimes his ideas and mine get intertwined.

Dan has his own question: "If we were having this discussion three years from today, and you were looking back over those three years, what has to happen in your life, personally and professionally, for you to feel happy with your progress?"

It's similar to the lottery question in that it gets people to project where they want to go and who they want to be. Dan said that you want to be around people who have a dream and stay away from those who don't.

My father always said, "If you tell me who your friends are, I'll tell you who you are." Sullivan takes that thinking to another level.

You want to be hanging out with dreamers and you want to achieve great dreams yourself.

I've never had a person not answer the lottery question. I think everyone has some kind of dream or goal, but it gets buried by the burdens of everyday life.

Disconnecting from reality is why the lottery question is so effective. It takes people away from their current situation and puts them in a fantasy world where they can start clean.

A Disneyland of the mind.

I don't play the lottery, but can see why so many do. They want an easy way to make dreams a reality.

I would prefer to earn my money through hard work and ingenuity, but if a one dollar ticket that allows me to purchase the Reds falls in my lap, I am going for it.

If people take the time to ask themselves both the lottery and Dan Sullivan questions, it will allow them to focus on their goals and objectives. Once they get focused on their dream, it may actually come true.

When I take over the Reds, tell me that you own this book, and I will cut you a deal on some season tickets.

When it comes to real lottery winners, the ones that seem to do best are those who sit back and don't let sudden money make them crazy.

One of my favorite stories is about a happy, but unknown lottery winner in Ohio in 2008 who took a deep breath and developed a comprehensive plan.

In my last book, I told lottery winners four things: Don't let anyone know you won. Set up a trust. Hire good attorneys and advisors. Take the money in annual payment.

On June 27, 2008, someone near Cincinnati collected a $196 million Mega Millions jackpot. The winner set their money up using the five concepts that I discuss in this book.

I felt like I had won the lottery myself. I'm not sure if the winner read my previous book or writings, but they followed my game plan.

According to the *Cincinnati Enquirer*, the ticket was sold in May, just outside of Cincinnati. Several weeks later, an attorney from the Cincinnati law firm of Graydon, Head and Richey claimed the ticket on behalf of an undisclosed client. A blind trust was set up and the winner opted for 26 annual payments of $7.5 million each. Because the identity was kept private, the winner won't have a posse of newfound "friends" looking for a handout.

The Cincinnati winner didn't rush to grab the money. They took their time and made a plan.

I've seen several winners (all who have run through their money) go straight to a car dealership and buy an expensive car BEFORE going to the lottery office and cashing their ticket. They couldn't wait to parade around and wave a large check. They also couldn't wait to blow all their money.

The Cincinnati winner bought the ticket in May, but it was not cashed until late June. The winner went to great lengths to protect their identity. The trust and advisors were put in place before the ticket was cashed.

We don't know the name of the winner. Ohio has an exception to the opens records law if lottery winnings are collected in a blind trust. The winner's name is only known to a few lottery officials, so they can see if the winner owes back taxes or child support.

Restrictions can be set up, and with good management, the money could be in their family for generations to come. The winner has a shot at maintaining wealth, since no one will know that they have it. They miss the thrill of acting stupid in public, but it is a great trade off. They won't have charities and leeches harassing them. They won't have the opportunity to establish "deep" bonding experiences with long lost friends and relatives.

Money can bring happiness to those who take their time, make a plan and do it right.

Handle your money in a way that will let you achieve your dreams

"Say, when this is all over
You'll be in clover
We'll go out and spend
All of your blue money, blue money. "
 -Van Morrison

"One fine day I'll find the way
To move from this old shack.
I'll hold my head up like a king
And I never never will look back.
Until that morning I'll work and slave
And I'll save every dime."
-Joe South

"Freedom is just another word for nothing left to lose"
-Janis Joplin (Kris Kristofferson)

Before you start working towards your dreams, you need to ask a hard question: Are you a saver or a spender? If you are spender, you need to keep focused on saving enough to truly achieve the dreams and things you desire.

The world is an increasingly complicated place, but one rule has held true for centuries: People who have financial security control the destiny of the people who don't.

As the late John Savage, a frequent speaker at the Million Dollar Round Table, said, "Spenders in the world always work for savers. It never happens the other way around."

The rich get richer for many reasons, but one is that they take a long-term view about their money.

I don't know if they have rehab for spending addicts. If not, someone ought to start one.

I was flipping through the news channels when I heard a guest demand that we not give tax rebates to poor people. "Rich people accumulate wealth. Poor people accumulate things," he said.

He had a trickle up theory of economics. He believed that poor people will go on wild spending sprees. The money will burn a hole in a poor person's pocket, while wealthy people would sock it away.

Most poor people need their income just to survive, but there are many who are broke because they don't handle money well.

There is a financial dividing line that separates savers and spenders. The savers wind up with wealth and the spenders wind up with debt. People on their way to wealth have good savings habits. People living beyond their means blow money on stuff they don't need.

Spending is instant gratification, like snorting cocaine. One shopper told me that she got a high from shopping like a high from drugs. Shopping doesn't work for me. When I walk into a store, my hatred of shopping contorts my face to resemble a mass murderer or a professional wrestler. People run out of the aisles when they see me. I buy what I came to find and get out as quickly as possible.

My goal is to accumulate wealth, not things.

When I was growing up, I used to think some people didn't have good jobs. They lived in rundown houses and often had their cars repossessed. I found out that they made as much money as my parents. Sometimes more. The people who lived in rundown houses spent money on gadgets they didn't use and motorboats that never made it in the water. They lent money to "family and friends" even though they should have been paying their own bills first. They had no sense of long-term planning and ultimately had no money.

Spending beyond your means is an addiction. A spending addiction is probably as hard to cure as a drug addiction. It requires changing lifestyles. I've frequently hired a casual laborer.

He is good at his craft and for 20 years made really good money. None of which he saved. Whenever I saw him, he talked about skiing trips, his bass boat or his brand new trucks.

When the economy turned, his house was foreclosed on and they repossessed his trucks. He has no savings or credit. His focus was on accumulating possessions. Now he doesn't have those possessions. Or any money either.

There is going to be a day when it all hits the fan. Americans are competing against workers in countries like China who have great savings habits.

Some argue that blowing money is a form of "financial freedom." I hate the J.G. Wentworth commercial where people are screaming "It's my money and I want it now." I hate it worse than the Cialis commercial where they are sitting in bathtubs in the middle of a field.

I have an obvious bias. I am in the business of setting up structured settlements for injured people. Wentworth is in the business of ripping them apart. I spent a lot of my time and my own money convincing some legislatures to regulate Wentworth and companies like it. We made it tougher on Wentworth, but they are still around.

Wentworth has an easy task. All they have to do is get people to focus on the immediate and forget about the future. I try to get them to focus on the long-term.

Wentworth and I have a different view of "financial freedom." Wentworth's idea of financial freedom is that you can get your hands on a wad of money and spend it immediately.

To me, real freedom means stability, security and independence. It means never running out of money. It means never having to work at a job you hate because you can't afford to quit. It means never becoming a slave to your creditors.

In short, it means having control and stability in your life.

That is what real financial freedom is about.

Not many people have true financial freedom. And many who have the opportunity to gain it screw it up.

There are a lot of financial choices in the world. Many companies prey on the "I want it now" mentality. Payday lenders, tax refund anticipation loans, car leases, subprime mortgages and credit cards are fairly recent additions to the world of personal finance.

All of those vendors will get you immediate cash—at a price to pay in the future.

Our grandparents didn't have access to quick money. Debt absolutely frightened them.

Maybe we should be frightened, too.

As Joe Nocera pointed out in *A Piece of the Action*, his classic history of personal finance, the rise of credit cards, mutual funds, 401(k) plans and individuals investing in the stock market are all things that have happened primarily since the mid-1960's.

Our parents lived in an era where they worked a lifetime at one company and got a monthly pension when they turned 65. Our children will switch jobs frequently and will need to depend on contributions and the investment results of 401(k) plans to allow them to retire.

Our parents and grandparents had systems to protect them. Our children and grandchildren are on their own.

I preach a simple gospel: Think about the long-term. Don't trust Wall Street, your government or your employer to take care of you.

Janis Joplin sang, "Freedom is just another word for nothing left to lose." Actually Janis, (and Kris Kristofferson, who wrote the song), had it semi-right.

Real freedom means living in a way where you can have fun, enjoy life and know that you are never going to hit a time when you are out of cash and out of luck.

Instead of, "It's my money and I want it now," a better way to think is, "It's my money and I want it always."

In the end, everything comes down to developing good habits.

I stumbled upon a fascinating academic article, entitled "The Ticket to Easy Street?
The Financial Consequences of Winning the Lottery."

In short, it asks the question, "Does throwing money at people solve financial problems or just push those problems down the road?

The paper gives empirical proof of two things that I've been saying for a long time: 1) Bailouts don't work, and 2) People who get large sums of money run through it in five years or less.

The professors came up with an ingenious and comprehensive method for their research. They obtained a list of winners of the Florida lottery Fantasy Five lotto game from April 1993 to November 2002.

They compared those names to Florida bankruptcy records to see how many of the winners filed bankruptcy and when. Filing bankruptcy means a person has completely hit bottom. You wouldn't expect that to happen to a lottery winner. Yet it does. Over and over again.

In the first couple of years after winning a jackpot, people who won small amounts were more likely to file than were people who won larger amounts. That makes sense. Someone with a large amount of money can initially weather a bad time or keep creditors at bay.

After three years, large winners are more like likely to file bankruptcy than small winners. Also, people who received large sums did not use that money to pay down debt or increase assets.

Winning the lottery did not help people increase their net worth. They needed to have set goals and an understanding of finance to make their lives better. It appears that they did not have those fundamental tools.

Giving someone a lump sum does not make financial problems go away. It's like putting an overweight person on a crash diet. Unless you can fix the underlying problem, they are going to fall back to their old habits.

This is true for lottery winners and the average American, too.

Hankins, Hoekstra and Skiba concluded that, "While we cannot be sure that homeowners or other beneficiaries of government aid would respond in the same way lottery winners did, the results may warrant some skepticism about the long-term efficacy of such a bailout."

Instead of looking at short-term solutions, people need to make long-term economic changes.

Otherwise, like the Florida lottery winners, we are going to wind up where we started from. Or worse.

Learn from my mistakes

I had my own bout of being a spending addict and being diverted from my long-term goals. I hope you learn not to do what I did at age 29.

I hit it big at an early age. I started my business at 23, and by 29 I had achieved the highest levels in the Million Dollar Round Table. I had a huge house in an upscale, gated neighborhood, a red Mercedes-Benz convertible and a big, penthouse-style office on the top floor of one of Lexington's taller towers. I was featured in *Forbes* and *Financial Planning*.

One year later both my lawyer and accountant recommended that I file for bankruptcy. My net worth had plummeted far into the red, and banks were breathing down my neck. My business was still going strong, but I had gotten into a real estate deal that I didn't truly understand with people I didn't know well. And it happened at a time when the market suddenly turned south.

Initially, I had grown my business by reinvesting profits and being frugal. I had lived modestly and had no debt. I knew my business backward and forward and spent a ton of money educating myself and my staff.

Suddenly, my cash was drained by a sideline investment and the expensive lifestyle I had decided to adopt. I didn't have the money to properly reinvest in my business and in continuing education. My focus went from a long-term view to just getting through the day.

I made the classic mistake of a successful entrepreneur. I thought my first success meant that I would be successful at everything. I got away from the things that had gotten me to the top.

If you study the history of entrepreneurs, you'll see that many do what I did. Their initial idea works. They become successful, but then get distracted with outside interests and start to lose the single-mindedness that made them a success.

Some recognize their mistakes and regain their focus. Others do not and their businesses fail.

I was lucky. I was able to see what I did wrong and make corrections.

The year was painful, but I learned lessons I will never forget. The experience was as valuable as a Harvard MBA, and I paid more than the school's tuition to achieve it.

I thought long and hard about what I needed, what I wanted, and the mistakes I had made. I sat near the lighted, uphill waterfall in my massive house, looked at my beautiful car, and realized the house and car weren't important. The only creature comforts I needed were an ice maker, cable television (this was pre-Internet), a recliner and air-conditioning.

What I really valued was financial independence and the challenge to be the best at what I did. I couldn't be independent if banks, creditors and a fancy lifestyle controlled my life. A line in Bill Hybels' book, *Christians in the Marketplace: Making Your Faith Work on the Job*, hit me. It essentially said, "If you spend all your time making money to support a material possession like a car, the car has replaced God in your life." Or as the band Zoe Speaks said several years after Hybels, "If money's our God, I want a new religion."

My religion had become keeping up my lifestyle and managing debt. Once I realized what I really valued—financial independence—it was easy to implement a different plan.

I ditched the big house and traded in the Mercedes for a Buick. I relocated my panoramic office to a small one on a ground floor. I sold most of the furniture in my home, except for the bed and recliner, and moved to a modest apartment that had air-conditioning, an ice maker and cable.

I read and reread *Pizza Tiger*, the biography of Tom Monaghan, the founder of Domino's Pizza. Monaghan's career path had the same sudden boom and sudden bust before he finally broke through to an international level. I couldn't afford to buy the book, so I kept checking it out of the public library. (I own two copies of it now.) Monaghan's story gave me hope and inspiration.

I eventually knocked out my debt as I reinvested in my business and education. I got a second master's degree in financial services and my fourth professional designation.

Going back to the original formula got me on a growth path again. Four years after I ignored the advice to file bankruptcy, I was out of debt and my business was bigger than ever.

"Stick to what you know" seems like common-sense advice, but I have watched many business people make the same mistake I did. Once things start to go well, entrepreneurs think success will last forever. They often get into ventures outside of their expertise and start spending too much money and time on a fancy lifestyle.

When they crash, they do one of two things: They give up and quit or they "double down," to use a gambling term, and focus harder on the original business. Like Monaghan did with Domino's Pizza. After he doubled down, his company reached success beyond his wildest dreams. He made millions, enough for him to buy the Detroit Tigers baseball team.

As I made my comeback, I used to play an obscure Jim Croce song, "Age," every single day. Two lines were my mantra: "And now I'm in my second circle and I'm headed for the top, I've learned a lot of things along the way. I'll be careful while I'm climbing because it hurts a lot to drop."

Some of the lessons I teach throughout the book, such as moving your money to a local bank and not having a boatload of debt, were learned through hard and painful experiences. Experiences I want others to avoid.

When people hit it big, they need to stick to what they know, live below their means and credit and put some money away for a rainy day.

Tools to protect your money

I talk about "getting rich slowly," immediate annuities and other ways to create and protect wealth in other sections of the book, but want people to have the concept of protection on their minds.

As Will Rogers said, "It's not return ON my money, but return OF my money that I am most concerned about."

In this lifetime, I want you to protect your access to money and give back to your community, but by moving your money off Wall Street to Main Street. If you read my previous book, *Wealth Without Wall Street*, you know I am not a fan of Wall Street banks, but there are practical reasons for moving to a small town bank or credit union.

I hope that you live long enough to achieve your economic dreams but if you don't, you need to get life insurance and also make sure you have a will. If you don't have a will, I hope you learn from my family's mistakes.

Move your money to a non-Wall Street bank or credit union

Most of us have an idea of what a small-town banker should be like. It's George Bailey, the character Jimmy Stewart played in *It's a Wonderful Life*.

We also have an idea of what a Wall Street "too big to fail" banker might look like. It's Gordon Gekko, the character Michael Douglas played in *Wall Street* and the sequel, *Money Never Sleeps*.

Although everyone wants to bank with George and no one wants to bank with Gordon, people keep winding up at Wall Street banks.

According to FDIC data from 2009, 57 percent of bank assets are with the top 20 banks. Thirty-eight percent of bank deposits went to the five largest banks, up dramatically from 1994 when only 13 percent of deposits went to the big five.

Why?

Big banks spend big money on advertising. The website *Business Insider War Room* combed through the annual reports of publicly traded companies and found that JP Morgan Chase spent $2.4 billion on advertising in 2010. Bank of America spent $1.9 billion, and Citigroup spent $1.6 billion.

The billions being spent in advertising would seem to casual observers to be the overwhelming factor in attracting customers, but that doesn't appear to the case.

New York Times opinion columnist Joe Nocera wrote an award-winning book, *A Piece of the Action*. Joe tracked the evolution of personal finance in America, including the credit card and banking industries. He cited research that said people picked their bank primarily because of its convenience to where they live or work. No other feature mattered. Very few consumers shopped for better interest rates, lower fees or better services.

Little has changed since Nocera wrote his book in 1994. A 2008 Compete.com survey asked 1,600 people who banked online about online and offline activities. The survey found that 52.6 percent gave "convenient location or ATM" as the reason they chose their bank. Less than 20 percent gave bank fees as the reason. And, despite the billions being pumped into advertising, only 6.3 percent said they chose their bank based on that factor.

Since Bank of America has 18,000 ATMs and 6,233 branches, more than any other bank, it would make sense that it attracts the most deposits. According to the *Wall Street Journal*, of the top fifty banks, $3.6 trillion was held by the four largest (Bank of America, JP Morgan Chase, Citigroup, and Wells Fargo) compared to $2.68 trillion held by the other 46 banks on the list.

Based on the data and history, getting people to move their money from a Wall Street bank to a possibly less convenient local bank would seem like an uphill challenge. But, at the beginning of 2010, Arianna Huffington and some of her friends decided to take on that challenge by creating the "Move Your Money" project.

There are some practical reasons for consumers to move their money. Moebs Services research shows that overdraft fees in 2009 averaged $35 for large banks compared to $25 for small banks. A similar gap existed with bounced check fees and stop-payment orders.

Personal service is another point in favor of small banks. According to J.D. Power and Associates (and quoted on the moveyourmoneyproject.org website), "Small banks have consistently rated higher in overall customer satisfaction than their Wall Street counterparts and that gap has only widened in the last few years."

Supporting small business is another benefit that Move Your Money touts.

According to FDIC data, 57 percent of bank assets are with the 20 largest banks, but only 28 percent of small business lending comes from that top 20. Small banks (defined as under $1 billion in assets) provide 34 percent of the loans, and mid-size banks (assets between $1 billion and $10 billion) provide 20 percent of the loans.

The data shows that moving money from a Wall Street bank has benefits for the consumer and for Main Street.

Wall Street banks have not learned much from their 2008 near-death experience. According to a report issued by the U.S. comptroller of the currency, in the fourth quarter of 2010, four of the biggest Wall Street banks held 95 percent of the derivatives for the entire banking industry.

In other words, JP Morgan Chase, Citigroup, Bank of America, and Goldman Sachs have 95 percent of the exposure to losses in the derivatives market. The other 6,349 banks in the United States have 5 percent.

It's stunning to see Wall Street banks go back into a derivatives market where they were burned so badly. It's like watching someone jump out of a sixth-floor window, survive the fall and go up to the eighth floor to try it again.

The next time they try it, I want to make sure none of my money is in one of their banks.

Managing risk with insurance

Insurance plays a key role in making sure that an illness, fire or accident does not put people out of business, and that the financial goals for families and charities are met if the person who set the goals dies before they are achieved.

I've been affiliated with the industry for 29 years. All of the titles behind my name—Chartered Life Underwriter, Chartered Financial Consultant, Masters in Financial Services, Certified Structured Settlement Consultant—have some relationship to the insurance industry.

I'm a licensed life insurance agent in several states and a licensed life and health insurance consultant in Kentucky, which means I can charge a fee instead of taking a commission for my advice. I'm also a licensed claims adjuster in Kentucky. Dealing with insurance claims is part of what I do in the structured settlement business.

I understand the power of life insurance.

The first life insurance check I ever delivered was on a 28-year-old family friend who was hit by a truck. The money allowed his family to bury him, hire a lawyer and eventually win a verdict against the trucking company.

A year later, the second death claim I filed was for my father, a 59-year-old who died of prostate cancer. I had argued with him for years before he agreed to buy the policy. He hated insurance. Near his death, he thanked me for convincing him to get the coverage.

I became a true believer in life insurance after Dad's death.

That makes me dramatically different from the rest of America.

According to the *Wall Street Journal*, "The number of individual life policies sold annually in the U.S. dropped 45 percent over the past 25 years, even as the number of households with children rose more than 25 percent. Meanwhile, the number of $2 million-plus policies, typically sold to affluent households, has been rising."

Wealthy people, who can afford first-rate advisors and attorneys, see the need for life insurance, but the message is not getting to Main Street.

I have theories as to why.

I've met a lot of quality insurance agents, really bright people who care about their clients and recommend innovative solutions. Many of them I've become acquainted with through the Million Dollar Round Table. No one, outside of their individual clients, knows much about them.

You don't see many reality shows about insurance agents.

If you asked the average person to describe a typical insurance agent, he would come up with a character such as the one Bill Murray kept punching in the movie *Groundhog Day*: a pushy, not-so-bright person more interested in making a sale than helping his clients.

I've been lucky to know people who have devoted their lives to the insurance industry and really know their stuff. Insurance advisors play an important role in people's lives, and agents should have the same kind of extended credentialing process and rigorous continuing education that certified public accountants have.

The perception of agents is one hurdle. Another obstacle is that the industry does not have a natural leader or public figure who stands out in the public's mind. Warren Buffett is a big player in the insurance industry, but the public thinks of him more as an investment guru.

The most recognized figures in the insurance industry have one thing in common: None of them are human.

Very few Americans can identify the president of any insurance company anywhere but most Americans can identify the GEICO Gecko, the AFLAC Duck and Snoopy from Peanuts, who advertises Met Life.

When an insurance company is faceless or is represented by comic figures or silly commercials, it is easy for it to be defined by negative stereotypes and bad claims practices.

Having an experienced and educated insurance advisor can make a huge difference. People need to choose an advisor based on professionalism and credentials, not because the agent plays golf with you or sings in the church choir.

Which is pretty good advice in picking any kind of advisor.

Why people need wills

"Everything we got, we got the hard way"
-Mary Chapin Carpenter

I have a will. I tell anyone who comes in my door to get one. No matter how old or young, rich or poor, I tell them they need a document that will specify what happens with their assets when they die.

With my background and experience, I should be the last person to be involved in an estate-planning nightmare. But I was when my mother and sister died.

Mom had a brain aneurysm and died unexpectedly on April 2, 2006. She never had a will, and no one ever really worried about it. Her only asset was our childhood home, and my sister and I were her only children. We would split the ownership of the house equally.

Only, things got a lot more complicated after Mom's death.

My sister and her 12-year-old daughter were living in the house when Mom died.My sister was coming off a period of unemployment in California as a single mother. She had no money. She didn't even have a bank account. She had just gotten a great job at Proctor and Gamble and was getting back on track after her years in California, which had drained her.

I was hit for a lot of estate expenses the moment that Mom died. I paid for her funeral, and I advanced the estate money to pay delinquent property taxes, some outstanding bills and the mortgage on Mom's house. I couldn't borrow money against Mom's house (it was owned by the estate, not me), so I had to pay the expenses from my personal assets.

My sister and I worked out a deal. When the estate settled, we would get an appraisal and I would buy the house at the appraised cost.

After I mortgaged the house, I could get back the money I had advanced to the estate. Her share of the house equity would give her cash to rent the house from me until her daughter graduated from high school. That would give her time to save up and buy the house from me and keep it in the family.

We never wrote anything down, but we trusted each other and it seemed like a good plan. And it was—until my sister fell down a flight of steps and died in October 2006. She did not have a will, either.

I knew she had a minor child and an adult son. What I didn't know was that she still had a husband.

She had been married to this man for several years, and her younger child was his. However, she had told us she had divorced him several years earlier. They didn't live together and, for most of that time, she had lived in California and he had lived in Cincinnati.

He came to her funeral, which I had arranged and paid for, and though he said hello, we didn't really talk.

Two days later, he had a lawyer file papers asking that he be named the estate administrator.

I hired a lawyer and found another to represent my nephew (he had a different father), saying that my nephew should administer her estate.

After exhaustive research, it turned out my sister and her husband never filed for divorce. Thus, under Kentucky law, her husband was entitled to half of my sister's estate. My nephew and niece would split the other half.

Since Mom's estate had not settled, it also meant that her estranged husband and his lawyer (after several rounds in court, he and my nephew were named as co-administrators) suddenly became involved in decisions regarding my mother's estate. Also, my niece was a minor, and a guardian ad litem had to be appointed to protect her interest. The guardian ad litem (an attorney appointed by the court) also had to sign off on decisions about Mom's estate.

It was a tedious and expensive mess.

The only way to reach a solution was to put my childhood home on the market. I advanced another chunk of money to get it fixed up for sale. Since the real estate market was dropping, the house was slow to sell, and every time we wanted to change the price, it had to go through the round of lawyers and interested parties for approval. An offer early in 2007 was turned down. That offer turned out to be more than what the house finally sold for in December 2007.

The arguing back and forth caused a riff in the family over very little money. By the time the lawyers and other expenses (I got back the money I advanced) were paid, my share of my mother's estate was a small sum and my sister's estate received the same.

A bill from an attorney came in after Mom's estate had settled. I was so tired of dealing with everything that I paid it myself rather than reopening the estate. Thus, I lost money on the overall process.

The person who got the most money from my mother's estate was my former brother-in-law. My sister's estate received half of Mom's money, and he received half of my sister's estate. My nephew and niece split the other half of her estate.

My mother doted on her grandchildren, especially my sister's children, who had lived with her for part of their childhoods.

She would not have wanted my brother-in-law to get that money instead of her grandchildren. And preventing that from happening would have been easy and inexpensive.

My family's series of events was unusual, but unusual things happen every day.

Involving a lawyer would have solved most of the problems. If my sister and especially my mother had prepared simple wills, the process would have been smoother and the money would have gone to the right people. If my sister had actually gotten divorced instead of working out an informal agreement (my brother-in-law was good about paying child support), it would have prevented our post-funeral surprise.

Losing a family member is difficult. It is unfair to ask the people left behind to make decisions and guess at the deceased's intentions. Also, state laws don't always reflect a person's true intentions and have to be honored in the absence of a will providing differently.

I suspect people don't have wills because they don't want to think about death. According to a survey by Findlaw.com, a popular legal website, more than 60 percent of Americans don't have wills. As the Findlaw site notes: "A will is a basic component of estate planning. Among other things, it specifies how your assets will be distributed after you pass away and who will receive them. Without a will, the laws of the state and the decisions of a probate court may determine how your estate is distributed, who will care for your children if they are minors and so forth."

According to the same survey, only 25 percent of people between 25 and 34 have a will; fewer than 10 percent of people in the 18 to 24 age bracket have one.

People over 50 are more likely to think about wills. More than half of the people that age have them. As noted, my 67-year-old mother did not.

People may think that wills and attorneys are expensive. In the overall scheme of things, they really aren't. I gladly would have paid 10 times the average cost for my mother and sister to have had wills. And everyone (but my brother-in-law and the attorneys) would have come out way ahead.

Al Smith, a prototype of giving back to society, with Howard Fineman and Don

Rule Five: Give Some Back

Rule Five for Lottery Winners: *Use some of the money to give back to society.*

One of the Five Reasons People Blow Their Money: *Not having a purpose for their money.*

"I believe the key to happiness is someone to love, something to do and something to look forward to."
-Elvis Presley

The King had it right. If you can do the three things he outlined, you have won the lottery of life. The irony is that Presley was not able to practice what he preached.

Elvis died at age 43. At the end of his life, he didn't have a partner in love, didn't have much to do and didn't have much to look forward to. He turned to binge eating and pills to make it through the day.

Like many people, Elvis died while he was still breathing.

His life got too complicated and frazzled. He's one of the most famous and influential figures of the 20th century, but had some miserable final years. A lot of people want to be like Elvis, with the money, fame and Cadillacs, just like a lot of people want to win the lottery and live that lifestyle.

Elvis died young, like a lot of rock stars do. Most lottery winners run through their money in five years or less. I loved Elvis, but I would not trade my life for his.

When you study the wealthy people who are truly happy, most like Warren Buffett and Bill Gates used their money to give back to society. Just like Andrew Carnegie and John Rockefeller did in the first part of the 20th century.

Ironically, Carnegie, Rockefeller and Gates did not start out as good corporate citizens. It's hard to find three people that were more hated by their competitors.

To find a version of "the happiest billionaire," my best candidate is Bill Cook.

Lots of rich people talk the talk, but Cook, who died in 2011, was one who truly made a difference. By opening a resort and casino.

Cook was a self-made billionaire who lived in Bloomington, Indiana. He made his money in the medical device business.

He was totally unknown outside of the state of Indiana and liked it that way. *The Bill Cook Story*, a biography by Bob Hammel, gives insight into a billionaire who danced to the beat of a different drummer. He had hobbies like driving his friend John Mellencamp's tour bus. He invented his first medical device in a small apartment, moved to a small house and stayed in it for the rest of his life. He became a billionaire, but it never changed him.

Cook didn't spend much on housing, so the irony is that he sunk his money into the ultimate real estate white elephant: The West Baden and French Lick Hotels in French Lick, Indiana.

The West Baden had been a historic landmark falling on hard times and literally falling apart. The French Lick Hotel was also long in the tooth and the local unemployment rate in pre-recession 1996, shortly before the resort opened, was over 20 percent.

It was a dead facility in a dying town before Bill Cook ponied up millions to bring both the resort and city back to life in the pursuit of historic preservation and jobs for the community.

I found out about Bill Cook at an unusual time: my honeymoon.

I had been to French Lick, but never West Baden. My wife had never been either. She was a little disappointed that we didn't fly to a more exotic honeymoon destination until she got to the West Baden. Now she wants to go back every week.

It's hard to do better than the French Lick experience. Both hotels had the beauty and splendor of a European grand hotel. The service and the restaurants were outstanding and reasonably priced. The resort has three golf courses, with two considered top in the nation. It has a large casino, but it's also one of the rare resorts where you can avoid the casino easily if it is not what you are into.

Who I kept running into at West Baden was the ghost of Bill Cook.

Many of the employees at both hotels seemed to be history buffs and several had been at the resort since it re-opened in 2007. They all kept quoting or mentioning "Mr. Cook" with personal affection and reverence. Finally, Clarence, a bellman, filled me in on Mr. Cook, his history and his total devotion to making West Baden and French Lick world class hotels.

Clarence, who like all longtime employees knew Mr. Cook well, got me to buy the *The Bill Cook Story* and spent nearly an hour telling me about Cook's philosophies.

One that struck me in particular was Cook's idea that helping a person find a job was the most important thing you could do. It gave the job recipient self-esteem, it gave them a way to support themselves and support their families and it gave them hope and a chance to plan for the future.

Most of the jobs in the French Lick area are related to the resorts that Cook restored to their original glory. The jobs are held by people who are proud, skilled and glad to have them.

Bill Cook didn't get into the West Baden and French Lick projects to make money. He had all money he needed and hotels looked like white elephants. He got involved to preserve a historic property and make it a destination point.

If you are looking for a model on how to be rich, pick up the book on Bill Cook.

You don't have to be a billionaire to give back to society. Al Smith sold his newspaper chain for millions, but it took him a long time to get to prosperity.

Al is one of the most important people in my life. He is my role model, inspiration, father figure and friend. He gives back in a total and complete fashion. At age 85, he is still atoning for wasted years in his youth.

In his fascinating autobiography *Wordsmith*, Smith's writes with gut-wrenching honesty about how he overcame self-destruction. It might be one of the best books that anyone anywhere has written about overcoming the grips of alcohol addiction.

I knew Al's basic story. His drinking caused him to lose a scholarship to Vanderbilt and many jobs in New Orleans. He stumbled into a small town, Russellville, KY, as a reporter, found his way to an AA meeting and stopped drinking. He found a wonderful wife, created a blended family, bought a bunch of newspapers that he later sold for millions, was appointed by Jimmy Carter as head of the Appalachian Regional Commission and became one of our greatest Kentuckians.

It gets more complicated than that.

The sections of the book that I found spellbinding were Al's years in New Orleans and the early years in Russellville when he was working as a reporter and living in a sleeping-room hotel.

When I think of men who have overcome the depths of addiction, I often think of Johnny Cash. Al's book reminded me of Johnny Cash's music: stark, honest and deeply personal. And with the raw edge of a man who looked the devil in the eye and stared him down, but knows he is always just one drink away from falling back into the abyss.

In many ways, Al's journey was far harder than what Johnny went through. Johnny was a star before he fell into the depths of addiction. He had a lot of help. Johnny was married to a remarkable woman, June Carter Cash, and had a strong and supportive family.

Al didn't meet his remarkable woman and raise his family until after he had stopped drinking. He kicked the habit with the help of AA, his own determination and the support of a small community in Western Kentucky. He did it with a drive to make up for the years he had lost to alcohol.

I doubt many would have predicted that the tipsy reporter in the sleeping-room hotel in Russellville, Kentucky, would someday be a man of national and international influence.

There is a lesson all of us can learn from. The Bible says, "Whatever you did for the least of my brothers, you did for me." We can't throw people away. We never know when the addict might go on to make a significant contribution to society. Al was one of the least of our brothers. He has never forgotten and constantly gives back. He portrays in gripping detail how near the bottom he was.

Overcoming adversity seems to be a common theme for those inclined to give back to society. Once you hit the bottom like Al Smith, you are more inclined to give back to those who have not made the same climb.

Al came of age in a small town. Like John Mellencamp, "I've got nothing against the big town," and grew up in a suburb of Cincinnati. Having watched Wall Street meltdown in 2008, I started to appreciate the common sense values of people who live and work on Main Street in small towns.

Like James (J.T) Gilbert in my hometown of Richmond, KY.

J.T. is the kind of lawyer every small town should have. He spent 18 years as Chair of the Board of Regents at Eastern Kentucky University and even longer as city attorney for the neighboring city of Berea. Along the way, he became one of the nation's top trial lawyers.

Kentucky has its share of big time rural lawyers. Sam Davies in Barbourville and Richard Hay in Somerset are two of the best injury attorneys the nation has ever produced. It's easy to see why small town lawyers make it to the top. There is a feeling of grounding that people don't have being anonymous in large cities.

Pete Mahurin of Bowling Green, Kentucky, is the Executive Vice President of Hilliard Lyons, a regional investment firm. He has been one of their top brokers for many years. He owns or is a board member on several Kentucky banks in places like Cecilia, Albany and Mayfield. He and his wife Dixie completed a million dollar gift to their alma mater, Western Kentucky University, and fund many other charities.

He started life in Short Creek Kentucky with hopes, dreams and an incredible work ethic. "I grew up on a little scrub farm," Mahurin said. "My brother thought we were broke. I just thought we were temporarily out of money."

Over 70 years later, he made his fortune, but still maintains his enthusiasm for high achievement and hard work.

It's easy to see why some people might be distrustful of Wall Street based advisors. They all went to the same Ivy League schools, live in the same suburbs, talk to the same people and developed a lifestyle that never allows them to interact with ordinary people.

Mahurin is all about ordinary people. He grew up in Short Creek in Grayson County, Kentucky, and then graduated with a degree in physics from nearby Western Kentucky University. He taught high school physics before joining the investment world and has spent most of his life in Bowling Green.

Both wealthy and working class Americans seek Pete's advice. One on the wealthy side is Lexington, Kentucky Mayor Jim Gray, who asked Mahurin to sit on the board of the successful Gray Construction Company.

Pete has the common sense of a man who grew up in Short Creek and achieved higher than those from wealthy families and Ivy League pedigrees. What he did learn from childhood was that one has to seize opportunity when it is front of them.

Jim Gray passed along a story in Pete's own words:

"When I was young, all the little communities in my area had a baseball team. One Sunday afternoon, someone on the other team hit a little pop fly that at least three of us were close enough to catch. Three of us ran toward it and all stopped, waiting for another person to catch it. No one did, and the base runners ran around the bases. We lost.

"Fifty years later I realized why that memory remained fresh and bitter. It was not that we lost, or that an error was made. Losing because I failed to act stuck with me forever, while failures made attempting to execute faded away."

Gray said that Pete "represents patience to the point of painfulness. After he talks, often everyone will nod quietly in agreement, as if divine wisdom has been spoken."

I don't expect divine wisdom from my advisor, but I would like some common sense.

There are some people who don't let fame and money overshadow their core values. Carl Kremer is one of them.

Carl and I became close friends at Eastern Kentucky University. I thought his future was in politics. He ran my campaign for student body president and a year later, I ran his. I lost. He got 90 percent of the vote.

A guy who can get nine out of 10 people to agree ought to be President of the United States, but Carl had different ideas. He wanted to teach high school history and coach. He wanted to raise a close-knit family like the one he grew up in. His goals never wavered.

Carl married his college sweetheart, but the road toward his life's vision was bumpy. His son was born with a serious heart defect and was given little chance of survival. After several heart operations in Philadelphia, he made it.

Carl came to Cincinnati Moeller, one of the top high school sports programs in the United States. Professional sports are littered with Carl's former students. He was at the big time, but coaching tennis, a sport he knew absolutely nothing about.

Then the head basketball coach resigned midseason and Carl took over the team. He turned the basketball team into a national powerhouse.

Carl received numerous offers to climb the coaching ladder. Many big time college programs offered him positions, and it was obvious that Carl had what it took to coach a major program.

Every time he got an offer, we talked, but Carl always said no. The long hours and disrupting his family was not worth fame and glory.

Instead, Carl has happiness. When you see people like celebrities dying young or doing stupid things, maybe fame and fortune isn't all it is cracked up to be.

Matching your values and spending habits is a skill many don't have. People ought to look at the model Carl Kremer offers.

One of the reasons Carl has been successful is that he never forgot his roots. His father was a union bricklayer in Troy, Ohio, and he had five brothers and sisters. Another who never forgot his roots was Frank Haddad, Jr., Kentucky's greatest criminal attorney before his death in 1995.

Many people hate lawyers until they need one. As Thomas Wolfe said in *The Bonfires of the Vanities*, "a liberal is a conservative who has been arrested."

Haddad Jr., once declined a potential client, saying, "He doesn't need a lawyer; he needs a hacksaw." There were not many people too hopeless for Frank Haddad. People in serious legal trouble often found their way into Frank's Louisville office.

A biography of Washington trial lawyer Edward Bennett Williams was entitled *The Man to See*. In Kentucky, the man to see was definitely Frank Haddad. Frank was a friend of mine, but he had thousands of other friends too. His funeral in 1995 was one of the largest in Kentucky's history. He grew up poor, but when he died he was a multi-millionaire.

Frank was humble, but not afraid of anything. He was quick-witted with a magnetic personality. He had a great sense of who he was. I once called him on a trivial matter telling him that I needed his help. His immediate response was, "Don, you must really be in trouble if you need my help."

Frank was loyal to his friends both rich and poor. He surrounded himself with a number of talented lawyers, including his brother Robert Haddad. They did more free legal work than anyone I have ever met.

It would not be unusual to see a famous politician or millionaire sitting patiently in the law firm's lobby while the firm was doing pro bono work for a janitor or someone from Frank's old neighborhood.

If Frank couldn't help them, they probably did need a hacksaw.

My father was a professional gambler and owned bars. As a child, it would stun me to see men who had toiled all week in a steel mill or hard labor job come into a bar and gamble a week's pay in one night. The workers knew how to make money, but had no purpose for it.

People need to have a purpose. With their money and their lives. Otherwise, they are going to cut both of them short.

When it comes down to happiness, we want to live in a world with good people. Being a good person, good family member and living a productive life is a tremendous accomplishment.

On *The Daily Show*, Jon Stewart once asked Arianna Huffington, "Isn't living a normal, stable life a political statement?" Arianna's answer was at this point in history, people need to take action. Living a normal life is not enough. I disagree. Please note that I have been a *Huffington Post* contributor since 2008 and I don't disagree with Arianna often, but Stewart put his finger on the problem.

There aren't enough people living normal, stable lives. I've learned when people get large amounts of money, it doesn't cure happiness. It can often magnify problems. People need to focus on being grounded and developing a solid foundation.

Abraham Maslow developed a famous hierarchy of needs. Maslow believed that you couldn't advance to self-actualization until you had your physical, social and safety needs met.

No matter who you are or how much money you have, people can find satisfaction and happiness by being good role models for their family, friends and neighbors.

You don't need to win the lottery to make that happen.

Getting by with a little help from my friends. Some of the people who gathered to celebrate Don's 30th anniversary in the financial business. All are mentioned in the acknowledgements.

Acknowledgments

"Thanks to you
I'm getting the applause"
-Johnny Cash

I dedicate this book to my grandson Liam Bigler, who was on the way to being born when I wrote the bestselling *Wealth Without Wall Street* book, which was dedicated to his sister Adelaide Bigler.

Since having supportive friends is a major theme of the book, it is fitting that I dedicate it to the men who participated in my June 2012 wedding: Clay Bigler, Nick McNay, Mike Behler, Lee Gentry, Bob Babbage and David Grise. They have stood by me for decades.

I dedicated my last book to my fiancée Karen Thomas. She is now my wife, Karen McNay. She is one of the top school principals in Kentucky (I have an extreme bias, but outside sources confirm). She is loyal, loving, intuitive and extremely intelligent. Growing up on a dairy farm, she is not afraid of hard work and is capable of love with undying devotion.

I adopted my daughters, Gena Bigler and Angela Luhys, after they were adults. Angela brought me my first grandchild, Abijah Luhys. Gena and her husband Clay brought Adelaide and Liam into my life. Both Gena and Angela have leadership roles at the McNay Group (**www.mcnay.com**), and Clay serves as company president. Some people hire a great organization. I adopted one and love them dearly.

Gena started writing a very popular "smart money" column for KYForward.com, under the tutelage of legendary editor Judy Clabes. Many have said that Gena is the best writer in the family. Probably so. Gena, Clay and especially my daughter Angela have terrific story ideas and many have wound up in my book.

Another aspiring writer in my family is my stepdaughter, Emily Kirby. She and her brothers Max and Zach joined my life when I married Karen.

I write about Al Smith in this book and dedicated my last book to him. He and his wife Martha Helen need to be acknowledged every book for their love, loyalty and being wonderful role models for how life should be lived.

Two key people made this book happen: Anne Parton and Adam Turner.

Anne Parton runs a business called iAssist. Anne has been a personal assistant to high-powered people around the United States, and I hired her to help me coordinate my last book tour. She was a major hit. She coordinated the writing of this book, contributed several key ideas, supervised the editing and promotion process and organized many aspects of my life. She is very bright, insightful, intensely loyal, has a great work ethic and is the ultimate professional.

She also supervises Adam Turner, who edited this book. I asked Liz Hansen, Chair of the Communications Department at Eastern Kentucky University, to recommend a college student who might want to intern with me. One of her recommendations was Adam, a senior honors student who is an editor at the Eastern Progress, where I got my writing start years before Adam was born. Adam can do it all. A terrific copy editor who has the looks, demeanor and intelligence to be a network news anchor. I'll do my best to make sure he gets there.

Two new friends have made important contributions to my book and life. Be looking for a book co-written by golf professional Clay Hamrick and me in the near future. Clay is an incredible golf instructor and has become a very good friend. Extremely bright, well-read and has insights on the world beyond sports. With his intense focus, Clay has turned me into a good golfer after a decade away from the sport. Another intelligent and insightful friend who has given me a number of column ideas is Dr. Rebecca Hammond. She, like my mother, made a late in life move into nursing, but, unlike my mom, kept going until she became a family doctor.

Louisville lawyer Jeffrey Stamper wrote to me a few years ago and said the grammatical errors were driving him crazy and volunteered to edit my columns for free. I took him up on it, and he has done a terrific job. Many of the details of those columns have wound up in this book.

I've been fortunate to befriend some of the best writers in America such as Gary Rivlin, Ed McClanahan, Byron Crawford, Dave Astor, Judy and Gene Clabes, Bill Robinson, Jack Brammer, Tom Eblen, Suzette Martinez Standring, Al Cross, Samantha Swindler, and Rick Robinson. Joe Nocera, opinion page editor for the *New York Times*, is quoted several times in the book and has been a wonderful friend and mentor.

From the broadcast world, Renee Shaw, Kelly Wallingford, Dave Baker, Ferrell Wellman, Jim LaBarbara, Joe Elliott, Tom Leach, Neil Middleton and Keith Yarber are friends whom I admire and learn from. I'm a frequent guest on Joe Elliott's show and we have terrific chemistry. I anchor election night coverage on Kelly's station. I was part of Tom Leach's morning show for three years and "the voice of the University of Kentucky Wildcats" remains a dear friend. I had several stints with stations that Keith Yarber ran before he left radio to start his Tops In Lex media empire.

I've attempted to shorten the acknowledgements (and hope people mentioned in the previous books understand), but the following people deserve a shout out in making this effort happen: Peter Perlman, Pierce Hamblin, Robb Jones, Bill Garmer, Rena Baer, Ben Chandler, Jennifer Chandler, Larry Doker, Donna Davis, Ivan "Buzz" Beltz, Tom Sweeney, Shelia Holdt, Richard Hay, Debbie Fickett-Wilbar, Sam Davies, Linda Davies, Samuel Davies, Yvonne Yelton, Laura Babbage, Keen Babbage, Carla Wade, Jack Brammer, Stephenie Steitzer, Whitney Sisson, Len Press, Lil Press, Steve O Brien, Billy and Annette Daniels, Randy Campbell, Bill Walters, Carroll and Janice Crouch, Dr. Phil and Nancy Hoffman, Luke Martinez, Dr. Jim Roach, Harry and Kerrie Moberly, Adam and Nathan Collins, Dr. Skip Daugherty, Wes Browne, Phil Taliaferro, Joe Greathouse, Shannon Ragland, Hans Poppe, Gary Hillerich and Len Blonder.

My wife's favorite film is *It's a Wonderful Life*, and the last line of the movie is, "No one is poor who has friends."

The theme of this book should be, "No one is poor who has real and trusting friends."

I won the lottery on that front.

Don McNay, CLU, ChFC, MSFS, CSSC

Don McNay, CLU, ChFC, MSFS, CSSC
Best-Selling Author, Syndicated Columnist, Financial Consultant
www.donmcnay.com

Don McNay, a financial consultant and award-winning writer, is an expert on managing money and one of the world's leading authorities on how lottery winners handle their winnings.

His syndicated financial column appears regularly in *The Huffington Post* and in hundreds of publications worldwide. McNay also has appeared in several hundred television and radio programs, including *CBS Morning News*, *CBS Evening News with Katie Couric*, *ABC News Radio*, *BBC News*, *KPCC- Los Angeles*, *WLW-AM-Cincinnati*, *Al Jazeera-English*, *CBC Television* (Canada), *CTV* (Canada) and *Radio Live* (New Zealand).

His insight has been sought by hundreds of print publications, including the *Los Angeles Times*, *USA Today* and *Forbes*.

Life Lessons from the Lottery: Protecting Your Money in a Scary World is McNay's fourth book. Two previous books, *Wealth Without Wall Street* and *Son of a Son of a Gambler: Winners, Losers and What to Do When You Win the Lottery*, have been number one Amazon bestsellers in a number of business and investing related categories.

Entering the financial services business in 1982, McNay was a pioneer in the field of structured settlements, helping injury victims and lottery winners handle large sums of money.

He founded McNay Settlement Group Inc., which is part of the McNay Group (www.mcnay.com). The organization is considered one of the world's leading experts concerning structured settlements, mass torts and qualified settlement funds. His company has been noted for its work with special-needs children, along with injury victims and lottery winners.

A graduate of Eastern Kentucky University, McNay was inducted into the Eastern Kentucky University Hall of Distinguished Alumni in 1998. McNay has a master's degree from Vanderbilt University and a second masters in Financial Services from the American College in Bryn Mawr, Pennsylvania.

McNay is a Lifetime and Quarter Century Member of the Million Dollar Round Table signifying that McNay met the organization's highly selective standards for service, production and ethical behavior in 25 different years.

McNay has four professional designations in the financial services field.

Don received the Certified Structured Settlement Consultant (CSSC) designation from a program affiliated with Notre Dame University. He is a Chartered Life Underwriter (CLU), a Chartered Financial Consultant (ChFC) and earned the Masters of Financial Services (MSFS) designation.

In 2000, McNay helped found the Kentucky Guardianship Administrators, which administers qualified settlement funds nationwide and serves as a court-appointed conservator for juveniles and incapacitated people. He is the owner of McNay Consulting, which provides advice for business owners. McNay is a fee-based insurance consultant for individuals and businesses in Kentucky and a licensed claims adjuster.

Among his professional involvements are former Treasurer of the National Society of Newspaper Columnists and former Director of the National Structured Settlement Trade Association. He has spoken numerous times at structured settlement industry conventions.

McNay has won several awards for his newspaper column, including "Best Columnist" from the Kentucky Press Association.

Don is a former Director of the Eastern Kentucky University National Alumni Association and served on the Advisory Council for the Eastern Kentucky University College of Business. He was named Outstanding Young Lexingtonian in 1985 by the Lexington Jaycees. He is an honorary Kentucky Colonel and named as an honorary Duke of Hazard by the Mayor of Hazard, Kentucky. He was in the initial group of people named to Legacy Society at Eastern Kentucky University and has served on the University's Planned Giving Committee. McNay is a University Fellow at Eastern Kentucky University and a University Fellow at the University of Kentucky.

McNay created the Ollie and Theresa McNay Endowed Memorial Scholarship at the Eastern Kentucky University College of Nursing after the death of his mother and sister in 2006.

A prolific author and lecturer, McNay has spoken to hundreds of legal and financial groups throughout the United States, Canada and Bermuda. He has published research articles in *Trial*, *Round The Table* (the official publication of the Million Dollar Round Table,) *Claims Magazine*, *Best's Review*, *Trial Diplomacy Journal*, *National Underwriter* and other financial industry publications.

Praise for Don McNay's best-selling book
Wealth Without Wall Street: A Main Street Guide to Making Money

"Don McNay is an original, provocative voice taking on all of those who would get rich off our ignorance and feelings of financial desperation."
--Gary Rivlin, *Newsweek/Daily Beast,* **author of** *BROKE, USA*

"Don McNay understands money...how to make it and, better yet, how to hang onto it. Read his book. It goes down easy, and it will do you a world of good."
--Ed McClanahan, author of *The Natural Man, Famous People I Have Known* **and others**

"At last, a road atlas to wealth for those of us who don't like driving on Wall Street."
--Byron Crawford, award-winning columnist, author, broadcaster and member of the Kentucky Journalism Hall of Fame

"Wealth Without Wall Street offers plainspoken advice from financial columnist and expert Don McNay. His guidebook is a wealth-building road map based on his long-time experience as a respected financial consultant"
--Suzette Martinez Standring, syndicated columnist, *GateHouse News Service*

"In his third book, financial wizard Don McNay has penned an operator's manual to wealth creation in common sense language and terms. Known for his simple, yet insightful, approach to money management, Don's road map to financial security is a must-read for all Americans searching for practical, long-term solutions to debt reduction and elimination, entrepreneurship and wealth-building minus the high-stakes gamesmanship of Wall Street. Through decades of toil in the structured settlement and insurance industry and profound commentary lent to countless columns for newspapers and on-line national publications, Don has earned a strong reputation as a prolific voice and thinker on money matters. His penchant for communicating complex ideas and principles with familiar musical limericks and Southern colloquialisms entertains and delights readers, and better yet, leaves them knowing more. Don's latest work will not disappoint those looking for solid advice on banking their money and having more money to bank."
--Renee Shaw, producer/host, Kentucky Educational Television

"In an age where journalism about money comes mainly from Wall Street and its environs, millions of Americans could benefit from a Main Street perspective, in which Don McNay specializes, and he does it in entertaining fashion."
--Al Cross, director, Institute for Rural Journalism and Community Issues; associate extension professor, School of Journalism and Telecommunications, University of Kentucky

"I have known Don for 25 years and have enormous respect for his ability to find unique solutions to not only financial, but also other problems. We served on our association's board of directors (NSSTA), and Don was a voice for sanity when we were dealing with difficult issues (If only he were in Congress now). I have enjoyed reading all his work, and this book is no exception."
--Len Blonder, Los Angeles, California; two-time past president of the National Structured Settlement Trade Association

"Don McNay combines deep understanding of his subjects with straightforward, clear writing and plain ol' common sense to help all of us think more clearly about the big issues."

--Judy Clabes, editor, KyForward.com; former editor, *The Kentucky Post*; member of the Kentucky Journalism Hall of Fame

"Don McNay has nailed it. In our changing economic climate, this is a must-read. In a realistic way, he has taken a complicated subject and made it easy to understand."
--Jim LaBarbara, member of the Radio/Television Broadcasters Hall of Fame, author of *The Music Professor, a Memoir*

"Don understands money, but his real strength is understanding people. He has real insight into what motivates the players and he explains it well to my audience. He's one of my favorite guests."
--Joe Elliott, Louisville, Kentucky; *The Joe Elliott Show*

"You don't have to study the labor disputes in professional sports, the misdeeds in college sports or the politics in Washington for very long to see there's a shortage of common sense. That's exactly what I found when I started reading Don McNay's columns several years ago. We brought him on our radio show at that time to talk about financial issues in a way that connected with people more than someone looking to come up with a great sound bite."
--Tom Leach, radio host and two-time winner of the Eclipse Award for broadcasting excellence

"Don McNay explains Wall Street in a way that's both relevant and readable. Don't be intimidated by his 'structured settlement consultant' title. Reading Don's work is like having a conversation with an old friend; an old friend who's as proud of his rock n' roll record collection as he is of his investment portfolio."
--Samantha Swindler, publisher and editor, *Tillamook* HEADLIGHT-HERALD, Tillamook, Oregon; winner of the 2010 Tom and Pat Gish Award for courage, integrity and tenacity in rural journalism

"Thank goodness the characters in my books have never gone to Don McNay for financial advice. It's nearly impossible to create conflict in characters who are prospering. Read WEALTH WITHOUT WALL STREET *or you may end up in one of my novels."*
--Rick Robinson, 2010 Independent Author of the Year for the political thriller *Manifest Destiny*

"Don McNay doesn't try to impress you with his knowledge; he cuts through all the Wall Street hyperbole and breaks it down into what matters most, dollars and 'sense.' His no-nonsense approach to money provides sensible, practical advice in a humorous fashion. He's one of my favorite guests, and I always learn something new."
--Neil Middleton, award-winning journalist, vice president of news WYMT-TV

"When Don McNay shares his remarkable experience and astute advice, as he does in Wealth Without Wall Street, *you can take it to the bank—literally. And you will be glad you did."*
--O. Leonard (Len) Press, founder, Kentucky Educational Television

"I have been a big fan of Don McNay's for many years. Don's writing style is real pragmatic without the hyperbole. He writes for the everyday person in a style that's fun to read, with very sharp insights for everyday investors. Don has not been afraid to call out the big institutions, while sharing the benefits of terrific opportunities right in our own backyards. This is a great read."
--Keith Yarber, owner/founder, *Tops In Lex*

Don McNay's previous books are *Wealth Without Wall Street, Son of a Son of a Gambler: Winners, Losers and What to Do When You Win The Lottery* and *The Unbridled World of Ernie Fletcher*

Made in the USA
Middletown, DE
10 July 2016